# Bond

# Verbal Reasoning

## 10 Minute Tests

## 10–11+ years

**Frances Down**

**OXFORD**

UNIVERSITY PRESS

# TEST 1: **Similars and Opposites**

Underline the two words, one from each group, which are the most opposite in meaning.

**Example** (dawn, <u>early</u>, wake)   (<u>late</u>, stop, sunrise)

1   (<u>tidy</u>, dust, <u>clean</u>)   (neat, <u>scruffy</u>, brush)
2   (climb, <u>broad</u>, slender)   (<u>narrow</u>, wide, high)
3   (hearty, cough, <u>unwell</u>)   (strong, cold, <u>healthy</u>)
4   (<u>pale</u>, red, coloured)   (<u>flushed</u>, faint, whiten)

Find a word that is similar in meaning to the word in capital letters and that rhymes with the second word.

**Example** CABLE   tyre   <u>*wire*</u>

5   DEFEND   detect   *protect*
6   SLICE   fleece   *piece*
7   KNOT   sigh   *tie*
8   MINUTE   shiny   *tiny*

Underline the pair of words most opposite in meaning.

**Example** cup, mug       coffee, milk       <u>hot, cold</u>

9   <u>few, many</u>       some, any       lift, raise
10   silly, foolish       <u>stupid, sensible</u>       serious, kind
11   show, display       conceal, hide       <u>present, absent</u>
12   <u>far, near</u>       distant, horizon       planet, star

Underline the word in brackets closest in meaning to the word in capitals.

**Example** UNHAPPY   (unkind, death, laughter, <u>sad</u>, friendly)

13   QUIET   (almost, noisy, busy, <u>silence</u>, thought)
14   CLASS   (children, work, school, <u>lesson</u>, group)
15   TEAR   (shred, drop, <u>cries</u>, sad, prick)
16   QUERY   (answer, <u>question</u>, peculiar, same, reply)

Look at the pair of words on the left. Underline the one word in the brackets that goes with the word outside the brackets in the same way as the first two words go together.

**Example** good, better       bad, (naughty, worst, <u>worse</u>, nasty)

17   upset, cry       happy, (pleased, sad, growl, <u>laugh</u>)
18   left, right       for, (five, with, <u>against</u>, hand)
19   finger, wrist       toe, (foot, <u>ankle</u>, leg, nail)
20   reveal, show       retain, (return, get, stop, keep)

2

Total

# TEST 2: **Sorting Words**

Underline the one word in brackets which will go equally well with both the pairs of words outside the brackets.

**Example**  rush, attack     cost, fee     (price, hasten, strike, <u>charge</u>, money)

1   talon, pincer        scratch, tear        (rake, nail, foot, claw) ✓
2   even, flat           position, stage      (level, dull, horizontal, period) ✓
3   pour, empty out      end, furthest point  (overbalance, apex, tip, fall) ✓
4   site, situation      put, allocate        (location, place, circumstance, move) ✓
5   clean, clear         innocent, virtuous   (pure, not guilty, harmless, hygienic) ✓

Rearrange the muddled words in capital letters in the following sentences so that they make sense.

**Example**  There are sixty SNODCES ___seconds___ in a UTMINE ___minute___ .

6   She put the picnic KSATEB _Basket_ ✓ on the CHKTINE _KITCHEN_ table.
7   It is cold DSIOUET _outside_ ✓ so put your KJATCE _Jacket_ ✓ on.
8   Straight after our SHILENG _ENGLISH_ SNOLES _LESSON_ , we had French.
9   Our local BRALIYR _Library_ ✓ has a RAVIDE _VARIED_ selection of books.
10  In the OLOHSC _School_ ✓ holidays, we went PNIGMCA _CAMPING_ in Wales.

Rearrange the letters in capitals to make another word. The new word has something to do with the first two words or phrases.

**Example**  spot    soil      SAINT      ___STAIN___

11  prickle   splinter    NORTH    _Thorn_ ✓
12  clutch    grip        SCALP    _CLASP_
13  cry       complaint   TABLE    _BLEAT_
14  beat      pulse       BROTH    _Throb_ ✓
15  jeans     material    MINED    _Denim_ ✓

Find and underline the two words that need to change places for each sentence to make sense.

**Example**  She went to <u>letter</u> the <u>write</u>.

16  The door sign has fallen off the toilet.
17  You have arrived time in just for tea.
18  Why have you put your feet on the wrong shoes?
19  In a park, the storm bench was blown over.
20  The autumn fall during the <u>leaves</u>. ✓

10/20

Total

# TEST 3: Selecting Words

## Which one letter can be added to the front of all of these words to make new words?

**Example**   _C_are    _C_at    _C_rate    _C_all    _C_lip

1   R_age   R_ally   R_at   R_oar   R_each  ✓
2   ✓ice   ✓an   ✓alley   ✓omit   ✓ow   ✓
3   C_hunk   C_lash   C_hip   C_rush   C_raft  ✓
4   B_ash   B_align   B_utter   B_eat   B_ail   M

*3*

## Find two letters that will end the first word and start the second word.

**Example**   pas (_t a_) ste

5   squ (_i d_) ea  ✓
6   spa (_RE_) ally
7   twi (_S t_) op  ✓
8   bo (_t h_) orn  ✓

*6*

## Underline two words, one from each group, that go together to form a new word. The word in the first group always comes first.

**Example**   (hand, <u>green</u>, for)        (light, <u>house</u>, sure)

9    (fourth, pass, <u>trouble</u>)        (with, <u>some</u>, by)  ✓
10   (<u>in</u>, out, on)                  (too, shirt, <u>vest</u>)  ✓
11   (bear, bore, <u>be</u>)              (ring, gun, <u>for</u>)   before  begu<u>n</u>
12   (for, <u>end</u>, first)             (rest, <u>less</u>, tale)  ✓

*9*

## Underline the word in brackets that goes best with the words given outside the brackets.

**Example**   word, paragraph, sentence    (pen, cap, <u>letter</u>, top, stop)

13   road, street, avenue      (town, <u>lane</u>, footpath, car, walk)  ✓
14   toes, ankle, heel         (son, hand, stocking, <u>foot</u>, wrist)  ✓
15   ruler, rubber, pencil     (lesson, case, <u>pen</u>, book, school)  ✓
16   sandal, slipper, boot     (socks, glove, person, hat, <u>trainer</u>)  ✓

*13*

## Underline the one word in each group that **can be made** from the letters of the word in capital letters.

**Example**   CHAMPION   camping   notch   peach   cramp   <u>chimp</u>

17   PARTICLE   patch   <u>crate</u>   prick   letter   treat   ✓
18   MONSTER    mower   stare   <u>stone</u>   moist   stream  ✓
19   COUPLES    place   supple   plush   scoop   <u>slope</u>  ✓
20   FLOUNDER   drown   <u>folder</u>   friend   drain   floor  ✓

( 4 )

Total  17

# TEST 4: Finding Words

Test time: 0      5      10 minutes

Write the four-letter word hidden at the end of one word and the beginning of the next word. The order of the letters may not be changed.

**Example**    We had bats <u>and</u> balls.     _sand_

1    A long icicle <u>appeared</u> on her windowsill last night.    *leap*
2    The ghostly sound of each <u>owl</u> could be heard.    *howl*
3    My cousins have <u>stones</u> all around their pond.    *vest*
4    In an airport lounge any unattended par<u>cel</u> looks suspicious.   *cell*
5    Pour the crea<u>m into</u> the striped jug please.    *mint*

Find the three-letter word that can be added to the letters in capitals to make a new word. The new word will complete the sentence sensibly. Write the three-letter word.

**Example**    The cat sprang onto the MO.     _USE_

6    In our pond we have a WR feature.    _____
7    Maisy's VAGE has pretty thatched cottages.    *Village*
8    There is a zebra CROSG right by our school.    *crossing*
9    Toby's rabbit is white with red E.    *ears/eyes*
10    In class, we put up our hands before SKING.    *Asking*

Find a word that can be put in front of each of the following words to make a new, compound word.

**Example**    cast     fall     ward     pour     _down_

| 11 | market | model | natural | star | *super* |
| 12 | thing | how | what | body | *every* |
| 13 | witness | shadow | brow | ball | _____ |
| 14 | drop | coat | forest | bow | _____ |
| 15 | guard | boat | style | time | _____ |

Move one letter from the first word to the second word to make two new words.

**Example**    hunt     sip     _hut_    _snip_

| 16 | bread | tint | *bead* | *trint* |
| 17 | bung | amble | *bun* | *gamble* |
| 18 | want | pin | *wan* | *pint* |
| 19 | bridle | growing | *bride* | *growling* |
| 20 | whine | heart | _____ | _____ |

( 5 )

Total [      ]

If these words were put into alphabetical order, which word would come third?

1  called      curries      charge      colour      circle      _____

2  quaver      quarry      quilts      queen      quartz      _____

3  dragon      dreams      drowsy      drench      drinks      _____

4  planet      placed      palace      pandas      pillow      _____

5  galaxy      gables      garden      gained      gallop      _____

If $p = 10$, $q = 4$, $r = 3$, $s = 6$, $t = 2$ and $u = 24$, find the value of the following.

6  $(p + r) - s =$      _____

7  $ps =$      _____

8  $\left(\frac{u}{q}\right) \times s =$      _____

9  $(u - p) + (s - q) =$      _____

Using the same values as above, write the answers as letters.

10  $(u - q) - p =$      _____

11  $qrt =$      _____

12  $pr - s =$      _____

13  $q^2 - p =$      _____

14  $\frac{qs}{u} + t =$      _____

15  $\frac{s + u}{p} =$      _____

If $A = 1$, $E = 2$, $L = 3$, $P = 4$, $S = 5$ and $T = 6$, find the values of these words when the letters are added together.

16  PLEASE      _____

17  PLEAT      _____

18  LEAST      _____

19  STAPLE      _____

Using the same values as above, work out the value of this calculation.

20  LAPSE – PALE      _____

Total

Look at the first group of three words. The word in the middle has been made from the two other words. Complete the second group of three words in the same way, making a new word in the middle of the group.

**Example**  PAIN   INTO   TOOK      ALSO   _SOON_   ONLY

| 1 | GRIN | GRIP | PINK | PLUG | _Plan_ | NAVE |
| 2 | TIME | MILK | LOOK | SLED | _else_ | SORE |
| 3 | PAST | SPOT | TORN | ROTA | _TRAY_ | YAWN |
| 4 | DUMB | BULB | LOBE | LAWN | _NAVE_ | VEER |

Change the first word into the last word by changing one letter at a time and making two new, different words in the middle.

**Example**  CASE   _CASH_   _WASH_   WISH

| 5 | ZOOM | _Loom_ | _look_ | LOCK |
| 6 | TUBE | _cube_ | _cure_ | CARE |
| 7 | GOAT | _boat_ | _beat_ | BEAN |
| 8 | SORT | _fort_ | _form_ | FIRM |
| 9 | DIET | _P,_ | _____ | PART |
| 10 | TIME | _tame_ | _same_ | SAFE |

Change the first word of the third pair in the same way as the other pairs to give a new word.

**Example**  bind, hind    bare, hare    but, _hut_

| 11 | rage, role | page, pole | sage, _sole_ |
| 12 | lead, loud | tear, tour | beat, _bout_ |
| 13 | shaves, have | tablet, able | misled, _isle_ |
| 14 | stream, team | chrome, home | stroll, _toll_ |

Find the missing number by using the two numbers outside the brackets in the same way as the other sets of numbers.

**Example**  2 [8] 4    3[18]6    5 [_25_] 5

| 15 | 7 [28] 4 | 6 [18] 3 | 9 [_45_] 5 | 16 | 4 [10] 1 | 3 [18] 6 | 5 [_24_] 7 |
| 17 | 7 [1] 7 | 6 [2] 3 | 12 [_3_] 4 | 18 | 5 [10] 4 | 3 [14] 8 | 2 [_15_] 6 |
| 19 | 4 [7] 3 | 9 [17] 8 | 11 [_11_] 6 | 20 | 6 [10] 2 | 5 [12] 3 | 2 [__] 1 |

7

Total

# TEST 7: Logic

*Help Test*

**Tom had six lessons in different classrooms. Match the lessons he studied with the six unshaded rooms.**

Tom studied English in a classroom with a lower number than the one he used for French.

*Scien.*

| 5 | 4 | 3 | 2 | 1 |
|---|---|---|---|---|

C O R R I D O R

| 10 | 9 | 8 | 7 | 6 |
|----|---|---|---|---|

History was in the classroom, directly across the corridor, opposite the classroom for Geography.

Maths was in between and next door to Geography and Science.

**1–6**   Room 1 = *English*   Room 3 = *Geography*   Room 4 = *Maths*

Room 5 = *Science*   Room 7 = *history*   Room 8 = *French*

**From the information supplied, answer the questions.**

An explorer was in a dilemma. He needed to travel north-west to his camp. In between was a large crocodile infested swamp. If he travelled north and then west, he had to go over a mountain range. If he travelled west and then north, he would encounter a fierce tribe of natives.

What would the explorer encounter:

**7**   south of the camp? _____    **8**   east of the camp? _____

In which direction would the explorer have to start to go if he decided to:

**9**   go over the mountains towards the camp? _____

**10**   go past the fierce tribe towards the camp? _____

**11**   go through the swamp towards the camp? _____

**Class 6S were collecting information to make a graph on the pets owned by the class.**

Rabbits were owned by Darren, William, Sita, Jane and Phil.
Sita, Brett, Jane and Sven all had goldfish. All those who owned a goldfish also had a cat, except Sven. William and Darren also had a dog.
Sandy, William and Brett each had a gerbil. Phil and Sita had a tortoise.

✓ **12**   How many types of pet are mentioned?   *6*

✓ **13–14**   What pets does Darren have?   *Rabbit*    *dog*

✓ **15**   How many children are mentioned?   *8*

✓ **16–17**   Which two children only have one pet each?   *Sven*    *Sandy*

✓ **18**   Who has a dog and a gerbil?   *William*

✓ **19**   Who has a cat and a gerbil?   *Brett*

✓ **20**   Who has the most pets?   *Sita*

Total

The code for the word COMPUTER is 72384169. Encode each of these words using the same code.

**1** TRUE ___1946___

**2** RUMP ___9138___

Decode these words using the same code as above.

**3** 3296 ___MORE___

**4** 8291 ___PORT___

If the code for SPENT is ORJAZ, what word is:

**5** AJOZ ___NEST___

**6** OZJR ___STEP___

If the code for CALMER is $+x£−@, what would be the code for:

**7** MALE ___−+x@___

**8** RACE ___+£f@___

Match the right word to each code given below.
TEST    MAST    TAME    STEM

**9** 4617 _____    **10** 4734 _____

**11** 3471 _____    **12** 1634 _____

Decode these words using the same code as above.

**13** 7634 _____    **14** 1764 _____

Here are the codes for four words.
9mQ%    mX%3    3Xm9    %Qm9
Match the right code to each word.

**15** TURN _____    **16** RATS _____

**17** STAR _____    **18** NUTS _____

Encode these words using the same code as above.

**19** STUNT _____

**20** SATURN _____

Total _____

A B C D E F G H I J K L M N O P Q R S T U V W X Y Z

The word FOOTBALL is written in a code as GPPUCBMM.
Using the same code:

**1**   encode the word SOCCER.   _____

**2**   decode HPBM.   _____

The word TYPE is written in code as VARG. Encode these words using the same code.

**3**   JAM   _____

**4**   ZEBRA   _____

The word FAST is written in code as CXPQ. Encode these words using the same code.

**5**   TABLE   _____

**6**   PINK   _____

Decode these words using the same code as above.

**7**   MXOQ   _____

**8**   GXAB   _____

The word BEAD is written in code as 2514. Encode these words using the same code.

**9**   FEED   _____

**10**   CAGE   _____

**11**   HEAD   _____

Decode these words using the same code as above.

**12**   6135   _____     **13**   85475   _____

**14**   If the code for RIGHT is WNLMY, what is the code for LEFT? _____

The code for the word BLACK is eodfn. Using the same code, pick the correct codes for these words.
sodq     odun     edun     sodb

**15**   BARK   _____     **16**   PLAY   _____

**17**   LARK   _____     **18**   PLAN   _____

Decode these words using the same code as above.

**19**   elug   _____     **20**   iohz   _____

(10)

*Time for a break! Go to Puzzle Page 42* ▶

Total _____

Complete the following sentences in the best way by choosing one word from each set of brackets.

**Example**    Tall is to (tree, <u>short</u>, colour) as narrow is to (thin, white, <u>wide</u>).

**1**    Ostrich is to (egg, bird, Africa) as fly is to (insect, sky, soar).

**2**    Speak is to (talk, mouth, word) as pace is to (stripe, stride, stand).

**3**    Hilarious is to (miserable, funny, comforting) as tragic is to (alive, fantastic, sad).

A B C D E F G H I J K L M N O P Q R S T U V W X Y Z

Fill in the missing letters and numbers. The alphabet has been written out to help you.

**Example**    AB is to CD as PQ is to  <u>RS</u>  .

**4**    PON is to MLK as JIH is to _____.     **5**    FD is to HF as JH is to _____.

**6**    Ah is to Dk as Gn is to _____.     **7**    Z11 is to X10 as V9 is to _____.

**8**    M12N is to O14p as Q16R is to _____.     **9**    aZ is to bY as cX is to _____.

**10**    AF is to CH as EJ is to _____.

A B C D E F G H I J K L M N O P Q R S T U V W X Y Z

Give the two missing groups of letters and numbers in the following sequences. The alphabet has been written out to help you.

**Example**    CQ    DP    EQ    FP    <u>GQ</u>    <u>HP</u>

| | | | | | | | | |
|---|---|---|---|---|---|---|---|---|
| **11** | 10 | 4 | 20 | 6 | ____ | ____ | | |
| **12** | Ab | Cd | Ef | Gh | ____ | ____ | | |
| **13** | 33 | zz | 22 | yy | ____ | ____ | | |
| **14** | 15m | 18p | 21s | 24v | ____ | ____ | | |
| **15** | ____ | ____ | 8 | 16 | 32 | 64 | | |
| **16** | 6 | ____ | 12 | 8 | ____ | 12 | 24 | 16 |
| **17** | ____ | 2 | 4 | ____ | 6 | 8 | 8 | 16 |
| **18** | a3Z | b5Y | ____ | ____ | e11V | f13U | g15T | h17S |
| **19** | ____ | ____ | 16 | 15 | 20 | 18 | 24 | 21 |
| **20** | 3Z | ____ | 6X | ____ | 13V | 18U | 24T | 31S |

Total

Look at these groups of words.

| A | B | C | D | E |
|---|---|---|---|---|
| rugby | iron | eagle | scarlet | rain |
| netball | lead | penguin | orange | cloud |

Choose the correct group for each of these words below. Write in the group letter.

**1–5**   steel   _B_      flamingo _C_      hail   _E_

purple   _D_      azure   _E_      hockey   _A_

sun   _E_      seagull   _C_      platinum   _B_

football   _A_

Find two letters that will end the first word and start the second word.

**Example**   pas ( _t_ _a_ ) ste

**6**   cla ( _s_ _p_ ) oon      **7**   swlv ( _ _ _ _ ) ect

**8**   sty ( _l_ _e_ ) mon      **9**   varni ( _s_ _h_ ) out

**10**   pan ( _ _ _ _ ) icle

Remove one letter from the word in capital letters to leave a new word.
The meaning of the new word is given in the clue.

**Example**   AUNT      an insect      _ANT_

**11**   TABLE      a story      _Tale_

**12**   CLIMB      an arm or a leg      _limb_

**13**   BRIDLE      marries a groom      _Bride_

**14**   FOWL      a night bird      _owl_

**15**   STEEP      a pace      _step_

Underline the two words that are the odd ones out in the following groups of words.

**Example**   black   <u>king</u>   purple   green   <u>house</u>

| **16** | boot | <u>door</u> | slipper | <u>car</u> | snowshoe |
|---|---|---|---|---|---|
| **17** | <u>beetroot</u> | carrot | peach | <u>apple</u> | clementine |
| **18** | bear | camel | <u>salmon</u> | <u>crocodile</u> | mouse |
| **19** | <u>camera</u> | CD player | radio | tape recorder | <u>binoculars</u> |
| **20** | forest | <u>lake</u> | orchard | <u>pond</u> | wood |

Total

Underline the two words, one from each group, that are the closest in meaning.

**Example** (race, shop, <u>start</u>)      (finish, <u>begin</u>, end)

1    (appear, disappear, collapse)      (vanish, rebuild, apply)

2    (competent, competitor, companion)      (capable, enemy, canopy)

3    (blue, aquamarine, scarlet)      (black, beige, crimson)

4    (scamper, run, skip)      (hop, scurry, scrounge)

5    (rubbish, wasteful, skip)      (dust, wasteland, uneconomical)

Write the four-letter word hidden at the end of one word and the beginning of the next word. The order of the letters may not be changed.

**Example**  We had ba<u>ts and</u> balls.                    *sand*

6    Please remember you must open each window slowly.    _____

7    I avoided the girl who made me cry.                    _____

8    The rope bridge swung in the breeze.                    _____

9    Explorers make epic journeys across the globe.    _____

10    Tom's ball dented the wing of his father's car.    _____

From the information supplied, underline the one statement below it that must be true.

11    Butter is a dairy product. Dairy products are made from milk.

    **A** Butter is made from milk.  **C** Dairy products are yellow.

    **B** Milk comes from cows.    **D** Cheese is a dairy product.

Find the letter which will end the first word and start the second word.

**Example**  peac ( _h_ ) ome

12    buil (___) rown          13    stam (___) roud

14    twic (___) ndure        15    dais (___) earn

If A = 5, S = 4, T = 3, R = 2 and E = 1, find the values of the following words when the letters are added together.

16    RAT          _____        17    EAR          _____

18    STAR        _____        19    REST        _____

20    STARE      _____

Total

Here are the number codes for four words.
3256   3526   6225   5223
Match the right code to each word.

**1**   FROM   _____     **2**   ROOF   _____

**3**   FORM   _____     **4**   MOOR   _____

**5**   Using the same code, decode 5226   _____

Write the four-letter word hidden at the end of one word and the beginning of the next word. The order of the letters may not be changed.

**Example**   We had bat<u>s and</u> balls.                              *sand*

**6**    I was stung by a wasp in my garden.                    _____

**7**    In the dusk the nightingales were singing.          _____

**8**    The team stays in cheap hotels to save money.   _____

**9**    The tide tugged at the tarred rope holding the anchor.   _____

**10**   Ben and his friends ate three loaves of bread.    _____

Find a word that is similar in meaning to the word in capital letters and that rhymes with the second word.

**Example**   CABLE       tyre           *wire*

**11**   DIVIDE      hair           _____

**12**   TALK        flat           _____

**13**   LABOUR      spoil          _____

**14**   ASCEND      rhyme          _____

**15**   SOIL        mirth          _____

Change the first word into the last word by changing one letter at a time, and making two new, different words in the middle.

**Example**   CASE     *CASH*        *WASH*        WISH

**16**   FLIT     _____   _____   PLAN

**17**   BUSY     _____   _____   BELT

**18**   PART     _____   _____   CORD

**19**   COIN     _____   _____   BARN

**20**   FLEX     _____   _____   BREW

Total _____

# TEST 14: **Mixed**

Rearrange the muddled words in capital letters in the following sentences so that they make sense.

**Example** There are sixty SNODCES _seconds_ in a UTMINE _minute_ .

**1** RAHSSK _____ are fierce predators that WDLEL _____ in the sea.

**2** Half of VYSNTEE _____ is YRTHTI _____ five.

**3** Myles prefers to play GBRYU _____ rather than BLFOOALT _____ .

**4** There are many SHMLSEEO _____ people on the London TSERETS _____ .

**5** The ISOTRHC _____ is the GELARTS _____ flightless bird.

Underline two words, one from each group, that go together to form a new word. The word in the first group always comes first.

**Example** (hand, <u>green</u>, for)  (light, <u>house</u>, sure)

**6** (kind, hard, for)  (beds, nurses, wards)  **7** (crack, break, mend)  (slow, fast, full)

**8** (grand, after, before)  (day, noon, hour)  **9** (pick, ball, match)  (stick, nick, miss)

**10** (water, free, tide)  (sun, fall, wave)

Find and underline the two words that need to change places for each sentence to make sense.

**Example** She went to <u>letter</u> the <u>write</u>.

**11** Please close the quietly door.

**12** Marion more one mark got than Jason.

**13** In the snow the dark was falling softly.

**14** Her shirt birthday present was the favourite.

**15** He likes to play Saturdays on football.

**BROTH  BROAD  BROOM  BROKE  BROOK**

If these words were written in alphabetical order which word would be:

**16** first? _____  **17** last? _____

Fill in the crossword so that all the words are included.

**18–20**  RARER  SUGAR
  SIDES  SAFER
  DRIER  FLING

15

Total

Complete the following sentences by selecting the most sensible word from each group of words given in the brackets. Underline the words selected.

**Example** The (<u>children</u>, boxes, foxes) carried the (houses, <u>books</u>, steps) home from the (greengrocer, <u>library</u>, factory).

**1** The footballer (picked, kicked, licked) the (ice cream, apple, ball) into the (back, stomach, heart) of the net.

**2** The business (deal, class, man) took his (newspaper, sandwiches, desk) out of his briefcase and began to (read, eat, write) it.

**3** (Why, Who, How) can I help you with your homework if (he, she, you) haven't brought your (books, cushions, hats) home?

**4** At midday the grandfather (clock, man, chair) in our hallway (chimes, jumps, talks) (two, eight, twelve) times.

**5** In order to (sleep, climb, write) neatly you will need to (eat, sharpen, break) your (pencil, knife, rubber).

Underline the one word in each group that **cannot be made** from the letters of the word in capital letters.

**Example** STATIONERY    stone    tyres    ration    <u>nation</u>    noisy

| | | | | | | |
|---|---|---|---|---|---|---|
| **6** | ELASTIC | stile | scale | steal | stick | slice |
| **7** | GRAPEFRUIT | pager | treat | tiger | grate | purge |
| **8** | SPLENDOUR | round | proud | unless | loner | drops |
| **9** | STRAIGHT | shirt | right | thirst | stride | tights |
| **10** | PLEASANT | least | stale | plane | nasal | please |

The code for the word BRIGHTER is 56174236. Encode each of these words using the same code.

**11** GRIT _____          **12** TRIBE _____

Decode these codes using the same code as above.

**13** 4365 _____    **14** 431742 _____    **15** 21736 _____

Give the two missing numbers in each sequence.

**Example**    CQ    DP    EQ    FP    <u>GQ</u>    <u>HP</u>

**16** 38   35   ___   29   ___   23     **17** 17   20   24   29   ___   ___

**18** 2   4   ___   16   32   ___     **19** 5   16   6   18   ___   ___   8   22

**20** ___   17   44   ___   33   21   22   23

( 16 )

Total

Fill in the crosswords so that all the words are included.

**1–3**

CHAIR   RADAR
MOTOR   CHASM
AWARD   AWAIT

| | A | | |

**4–6**

MEETS   SHEDS
SOCKS   OLIVE
CRIME   STORM

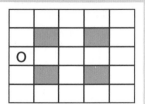

From the information supplied, underline the one statement below it that must be true.

**7**   My dustbin is black. My rubbish collection is on Thursdays.

   **A** All black dustbins are emptied on Thursdays.

   **B** My dustbin is emptied on Thursdays.

   **C** Thursday is a convenient day for rubbish collection.

   **D** My black dustbin is rubbish.

A B C D E F G H I J K L M N O P Q R S T U V W X Y Z

The word FLOWER is written in code as GMPXFS. Encode each of these words using the same code.

**8**   ROW   _____   **9**   LEAF   _____

**10**   Decode TVOOZ using the same code.   _____

Move one letter from the first word to the second word to make two new words.

| **Example** | hunt | sip | *hut* | *snip* |
|---|---|---|---|---|
| **11** | spear | teak | _____ | _____ |
| **12** | mange | hue | _____ | _____ |
| **13** | frail | stay | _____ | _____ |
| **14** | broom | led | _____ | _____ |
| **15** | tired | tout | _____ | _____ |

Write the four-letter word hidden at the end of one word and the beginning of the next word. The order of the letters may not be changed.

**Example**  We had bats _and_ balls.   *sand*

**16**   It was remarkable how fast army tanks appeared.   _____

**17**   The Australians batted until eleven o'clock.   _____

**18**   Watch out, there is a hair on that piece of cake!   _____

**19**   I wish chocolate fountains would flow all the time.   _____

**20**   I catch the school bus to my village every day.   _____

*Time for a break! Go to Puzzle Page 43* ▶

Total

Test time: 0    5    10 minutes

Look at these words. Sort them into groups.

**1–4**  Ford       metre       Berlin       pineapple
        Venice     Vauxhall    banana       millimetre

| A | B | C | D |
|---|---|---|---|
| Cars | Measurements | Cities | Fruit |
| _____ | _____ | _____ | _____ |
| _____ | _____ | _____ | _____ |

Add one letter to the word in capital letters to make a new word. The meaning of the new word is given in the clue.

**Example**  PLAN        simple        _____PLAIN_____

| **5** | CEASE | a fold in material | _____ |
| **6** | PLATE | the roof of your mouth | _____ |
| **7** | READ | not looking forward to | _____ |
| **8** | TAPER | to interfere with | _____ |

Underline the two words that are the odd ones out in the following groups of words.

**Example**  black  <u>king</u>  purple  green  <u>house</u>

**9**   ring   circle  necklace  bracelet  box       **10**   breakfast  lunch  cup    plate    dinner
**11**  finger  nail   tack      screw     shoe      **12**   bite       tooth  chew   munch    lip

Rearrange the letters in capitals to make another word. The new word has something to do with the first two words or phrases.

**Example**  spot        soil            SAINT        _____STAIN_____

| **13** | brown | breakfast bread | STOAT | _____ |
| **14** | mouldy | not fresh | LEAST | _____ |
| **15** | surplus | an extra one | REAPS | _____ |
| **16** | wall covering | covers a wound | STAPLER | _____ |

Complete the following sentences in the best way by choosing one word from each set of brackets.

**Example**  Tall is to (tree, <u>short</u>, colour) as narrow is to (thin, white, <u>wide</u>).

**17**   King is to (crown, queen, kingdom) as judge is to (wig, jury, bench).
**18**   Fish is to (cod, scales, chips) as bird is to (beak, wing, feathers).
**19**   Pig is to (sty, piglet, pork) as cow is to (steak, beef, milk).
**20**   Hammer is to (tool, nail, anvil) as spanner is to (screw, pin, nut).

( 18 )

Total

Underline one word in brackets that will go equally well with both the pairs of words outside the brackets.

**Example** (rush, attack) (cost, fee) (price, hasten, strike, <u>charge</u>, money)

| | | | |
|---|---|---|---|
| 1 | examine, inspect | stop, limit | (test, <u>check</u>, restrain, study) |
| 2 | correctly, properly | brim, rise | (right, <u>well</u>, simply, spring) |
| 3 | imitate, mirror | think, consider | (reflect, demonstrate, ponder, return) |
| 4 | boundary, edge | confine, curb | (margin, pavement, limit, restrict) |
| 5 | affordable, inexpensive | second-rate, inferior | (mean, reasonable, low, cheap) |

A B C D E F G H I J K L M N O P Q R S T U V W X Y Z

Fill in the missing letters. The alphabet has been written out to help you.

**Example** AB is to CD as PQ is to ___RS___.

6 ACF is to GIL as MOR is to _____.    7 ZX is to WU as TR is to _____.

8 ZA is to XC as VE is to _____.    9 ZW is to TQ as NK is to _____.

10 AmD is to GnJ as MoP is to _____.

In her basket, Amy had beans, carrots, cucumber, mushrooms and tomatoes. Work out which section of the supermarket shelves she found her items on.

**11–15**

TOP

| cabbage | B | C | celery | potatoes |
|---|---|---|---|---|
| A | onions | D | E | broccoli |

LEFT ... RIGHT

BOTTOM

Beans
Mushrooms

A = cucumb ✓
B = bens ✓
C = carrols ✓
D = Muswoars ✓
E = tomates ✓

The beans were somewhere above the mushrooms.
The cucumber was somewhere to the left of the tomatoes but not under the carrots.
The carrots, in turn, were directly above the mushrooms.

Look at the first group of three words. The word in the middle has been made from the two other words. Complete the second group of three words in the same way, making a new word in the middle of the group.

**Example** PAIN INTO TOOK    ALSO _SOON_ ONLY

| | | | | | | |
|---|---|---|---|---|---|---|
| 16 | SLAP | LACK | DOCK | PICK | ICED | HEED |
| 17 | SORT | STOP | OPEN | FEEL | flc x | OXEN |
| 18 | POOL | LOVE | SAVE | SEAL | la mb | LIMB |
| 19 | MASH | SALE | TEAL | WAGE | GaTe | PERT |
| 20 | FLAG | GLAD | DRAB | SLIP | PLuc | GRUB |

GULP
TEGA
LPGU

Total

Underline the two words, one from each group, which are the most opposite in meaning.

**Example** (dawn, <u>early</u>, wake)     (<u>late</u>, stop, sunrise)

**1**   (off, under, up)              (on, through, by)

**2**   (steaming, warm, icy)       (cool, sleet, cold)

**3**   (for, again, by)            (up, through, against)

**4**   (leave, grant, give)        (pull, apply, take)

**5**   (point, sharp, apex)        (notice, blunt, hill)

A B C D E F G H I J K L M N O P Q R S T U V W X Y Z

Give the two missing groups of letters in the following sequences. The alphabet has been written out to help you.

**Example** CQ    DP    EQ    FP    <u>GQ</u>   <u>HP</u>

**6**   AC     EG     IK     MO     QS     _____   _____

**7**   ZP     YQ     XR     WS     VT     _____   _____

**8**   CAD    DBE    ECF    FDG    GEH    _____   _____

**9**   AZ     CX     EV     GT     IR     _____   _____

**10**  feg    gfh    hgi    ihj    jik    _____   _____

Find the letter which will end the first word and start the second word.

**Example**  peac ( <u>h</u> ) ome

**11**   clea (___) eign          **12**   spac (___) njoy

**13**   tric (___) icks          **14**   rel (___) ell

**15**   tune (___) esk

Here are the number codes for four words.
9413   9471   7413   9331
Match the right code to each word.

**16**   LACK   _____          **17**   LAKE   _____

**18**   LEEK   _____          **19**   CAKE   _____

Decode this word using the same code as above.

**20**   1493   _____

Total

Write the four-letter word hidden at the end of one word and the beginning of the next word. The order of the letters may not be changed.

**Example**  We had bat<u>s and</u> balls.  <u>  sand  </u>

1  We saw nothing but desert stretching before us.  _____

2  Mrs Smith knelt down to dust under the table.  _____

3  Neither the zebra nor the antelope heard the lion.  _____

4  The pies are in the oven.  _____

5  Some people think taking vitamins helps stop illnesses spreading.  _____

From the information supplied, underline the one statement below it that must be true.

6  French is taught at our school. Our class has a French lesson on Friday.

    **A** All schools teach French.         **C** French is taught only on Friday.

    **B** We have a French lesson on Friday.   **D** Our school is in France.

The code for the word CLOTHES is written as @!+?/*£. Decode these words using the same code as above.

7  @+£?  _____      8  £@/++!  _____      9  @/**£*  _____

Encode these words using the same code as above.

10  HOTEL  _____      11  THOSE  _____

Complete the following sentences in the best way by choosing one word from each set of brackets.

**Example**  Tall is to (tree, <u>short</u>, colour) as narrow is to (thin, white, <u>wide</u>).

12  Pen is to (paper, write, biro) as brush is to (paint, blue, easel).

13  Wine is to bottle as (milk, petrol, meat) is to (mouth, garage, carton).

14  (Trousers, Top, Under) is to bottom as high is to (above, over, low).

15  Mind is to (think, read, care) as stomach is to (digest, fat, ache).

16  Go is to (get, come, stop) as green is to (amber, red, light).

If a = 5, b = 4, c = 3, d = 2 and e = 1, find the value of the following.

17  $(a + b) - (c + d)$ =  _____      18  $\dfrac{bc}{d}$ =  _____

19  $(d^2 + c^2) - e$ =  _____      20  $\dfrac{be}{d} + a$ =  _____

Total

Test time: 0        5        10 minutes

Find a word that is similar in meaning to the word in capital letters and that rhymes with the second word.

**Example** CABLE   tyre   ___wire___

| 1 | ENCLOSURE | dense | _____ | 2 | LIQUID | course | _____ |
| 3 | CONFUSE | cuddle | _____ | 4 | SHARE | mice | _____ |

Find a word that can be put in front of each of the following words to make a new, compound word.

**Example** cast   fall   word   pour   ___down___

| 5 | fall | mark | proof | colour | _____ |
| 6 | fighter | work | side | arm | _____ |
| 7 | man | drop | ball | flake | _____ |
| 8 | forest | drop | coat | bow | _____ |

If these words are placed in alphabetical order, which comes fourth?

| 9 | flatworm | flatbed | fledgling | flannel | flank | _____ |
| 10 | stagnant | stagecoach | stagger | stadium | stainless | _____ |
| 11 | harness | harmonic | harelip | harpoon | harrier | _____ |
| 12 | larder | larva | larceny | lapwing | largesse | _____ |

Find the three-letter word that can be added to the letters in capitals to make a new word. The new word will complete the sentence sensibly. Write the three-letter word.

**Example** The cat sprang onto the MO.                    ___USE___

| 13 | Our car has new tyres on each WH. | _____ |
| 14 | The headmaster said my H was too long and needed cutting. | _____ |
| 15 | There are not enough chairs so he is STING. | _____ |
| 16 | CRIES are a red fruit with a stone in the middle. | _____ |

A  B  C  D  E  F  G  H  I  J  K  L  M  N  O  P  Q  R  S  T  U  V  W  X  Y  Z

Give the two missing pairs of letters in the following sequences. The alphabet has been written out to help you.

**Example** CQ  DP  EQ  FP  _GQ_  _HP_

| 17 | AX | DU | GR | JO | ML | ___ ___ | 18 | WV | YX | AZ | CB | ED | ___ ___ |
| 19 | GQ | HQ | IR | JR | KS | ___ ___ | 20 | BW | BV | CU | CT | DS | ___ ___ |

Total

---

**Underline the pair of words most opposite in meaning.**

**Example** cup, mug     coffee, milk    <u>hot, cold</u>

| **1** | win, lose | win, success | failure, disappointment |
| **2** | hot, cool | warm, cool | cold, warm |
| **3** | clear, lucid | cloudy, rainy | clear, cloudy |
| **4** | stand, deliver | collect, deliver | send, deliver |

---

**Find the missing number by using the two numbers outside the brackets in the same way as the other sets of numbers.**

**Example**   2 [8] 4     3 [18] 6      5 [<u>25</u>] 5

| **5** | 7 [10] 1 | 3 [18] 5 | 4 [___] 2 |
| **6** | 14 [11] 4 | 13 [7] 7 | 12 [___] 3 |
| **7** | 5 [15] 2 | 7 [5] 6 | 4 [___] 3 |
| **8** | 6 [8] 7 | 7 [6] 4 | 8 [___] 3 |

---

**Underline the word the brackets which goes best with the words given outside the brackets.**

**Example** word, paragraph, sentence    (pen, cap, <u>letter</u>, top, stop)

| **9** | rush, dash, shoot | (arrow, dart, rifle, move, jog) |
| **10** | honest, light, just | (true, pale, dark, fair, time) |
| **11** | remove, expel, emit | (take, school, bully, reject, eject) |
| **12** | rotund, portly, heavy | (weight, harbour, stout, stone, round) |

---

**Move one letter from the first word to the second word to make two new words.**

**Example** hunt    sip    <u> hut </u>     <u> snip </u>

| **13** | crane | bed | _____ _____ | **14** | plight | car | _____ _____ |
| **15** | suet | urn | _____ _____ | **16** | flood | hit | _____ _____ |

---

**Underline the two words that are made from the same letters.**

**Example** TAP     PET     <u>TEA</u>     POT     <u>EAT</u>

| **17** | SHEARS | SHEEP | SHAPES | PHASES | SHORTS |
| **18** | STRONG | GRUNTS | GRANTS | STRAIN | STRUNG |
| **19** | STAPLE | PLEASE | PALEST | APPLES | SCRAPE |
| **20** | BLAST | STOLE | STALE | LABEL | LEAST |

Total

Look at these groups of words.

| A | B | C | D | E |
|---|---|---|---|---|
| pencil | oak | seaside | table | trout |
| ruler | elm | sandcastle | cupboard | carp |

Choose the correct group for each of these words below. Write in the group letter.

**1–5**  beech _____   rubber _____   perch _____   pike _____   beach _____

bed _____   pen _____   pine _____   chair _____   seaweed _____

Remove one letter from the word in capital letters to leave a new word.
The meaning of the new word is given in the clue.

**Example** AUNT        an insect        ___ANT___

**6**   FRAME        well known        _____

**7**   CHEAT        to make hotter        _____

**8**   PLANT        organise        _____

**9**   CRATER        supply        _____

**10**  LADDER        snake        _____

Underline the word in the brackets that is most opposite in meaning to the word in capitals.

**Example** WIDE        (broad, vague, long, <u>narrow</u>, motorway)

**11**  THIN        (thick, healthy, full, emaciated, skinny)

**12**  EASY        (simple, facile, difficult, descriptive, quick)

**13**  FULL        (avoid, replete, refill, empty, complete)

**14**  FLAT        (level, uneven, square, apartment, deflated)

**15**  QUIET        (noisy, quite, crowded, whispering, tranquil)

Underline the pair of words most similar in meaning.

**Example** come, go        <u>roams, wanders</u>        fear, fare

**16**  high, low        climb, ascend        lift, descend

**17**  polite, impolite        before, now        concur, agree

**18**  healthy, well        well, lake        health, happiness

**19**  dart, dodge        dodge, budge        arrow, dart

**20**  pillow, bed        carpet, rug        bucket, spade

Total

# Answers

## TEST 1: Similars and Opposites

1 tidy, scruffy
2 broad, narrow
3 unwell, healthy
4 pale, flushed
5 protect
6 piece
7 tie
8 tiny
9 few, many
10 stupid, sensible
11 present, absent
12 far, near
13 silence
14 group
15 shred
16 question
17 laugh
18 against
19 ankle
20 keep

## TEST 2: Sorting Words

1 claw
2 level
3 tip
4 place
5 pure
6 basket kitchen
7 outside jacket
8 English lesson
9 library varied
10 school camping
11 THORN
12 CLASP
13 BLEAT
14 THROB
15 DENIM
16 door toilet
17 time just
18 feet shoes
19 park storm
20 autumn leaves

## TEST 3: Selecting Words

1 r
2 v
3 c
4 m
5 id
6 re
7 st
8 th
9 troublesome
10 invest
11 begun
12 endless
13 lane
14 foot
15 pen
16 trainer
17 crate
18 stone
19 slope
20 folder

## TEST 4: Finding Words

1 leap
2 howl
3 vest
4 cell
5 mint
6 ATE
7 ILL
8 SIN
9 YES
10 PEA
11 super
12 some
13 eye
14 rain
15 life
16 bred taint
17 bun gamble
18 wan pint
19 bride growling
20 wine hearth

## TEST 5: Alphabetical Order and Substitution

1 circle
2 quaver
3 drench
4 pillow
5 galaxy
6 7
7 60
8 36
9 16
10 p
11 u
12 u
13 s
14 r
15 r
16 17
17 16
18 17
19 21
20 5

## TEST 6: Word Progressions

1 PLAN
2 ELSE
3 TRAY
4 NAVE
5 LOOM LOOK
6 CUBE CURE
7 BOAT BEAT
8 FORT FORM
9 DIRT DART
10 TAME SAME
11 sole
12 bout
13 isle
14 toll
15 45
16 24
17 3
18 4
19 17
20 1

## TEST 7: Logic

1 Room 1: English
2 Room 3: Geography
3 Room 4: Maths
4 Room 5: Science
5 Room 7: French
6 Room 8: History
7 tribe
8 mountains
9 north
10 west
11 north west
12 6 pets
13–14 rabbit and dog
15 8 children
16–17 Sandy and Sven
18 William
19 Brett
20 Sita

## TEST 8: Simple Codes

1 1946
2 9438
3 MORE
4 PORT
5 NEST
6 STEP
7 £+×–
8 @+$–
9 TAME
10 TEST
11 STEM
12 MAST
13 EAST
14 MEAT

15 mX%3
16 %Qm9
17 9mQ%
18 3Xm9
19 9mX3m
20 9QmX%3

## TEST 9: More Complicated Codes

1 TPDDFS
2 GOAL
3 LCO
4 BGDTC
5 QXYIB
6 MFKH
7 PART
8 JADE
9 6554
10 3175
11 8514
12 FACE
13 HEDGE
14 QJKY
15 edun
16 sodb
17 odun
18 sodq
19 BIRD
20 FLEW

## TEST 10: Sequences

1 bird    insect
2 talk    stride
3 funny   sad
4 GFE
5 LJ
6 Jq
7 T8
8 S18T
9 dW
10 GL
11 30    8
12 lj    Kl
13 ll    xx
14 27y   30D
15 2    4
16 4    18
17 2    4
18 c7X   d9W
19 12    12
20 4Y   9W

## TEST 11: Mixed

1–5
  B C E
  D D A
  E C B
  A
6 SP
7 EL
8 LE
9 SH
10 IC
11 TALE
12 LIMB
13 BRIDE
14 OWL
15 STEP
16 door, car
17 beetroot, carrot
18 salmon, crocodile
19 camera, binoculars
20 lake, pond

## TEST 12: Mixed

1 disappear, vanish
2 competent, capable
3 scarlet, crimson
4 scamper, scurry
5 wasteful, uneconomical
6 stop
7 whom
8 hero
9 keep
10 scar
11 A
12 D
13 P
14 E
15 Y
16 10
17 8
18 14
19 10
20 15

## TEST 13: **Mixed**

| | |
|---|---|
| **1** 3526 | **11** share |
| **2** 5223 | **12** chat |
| **3** 3256 | **13** toil |
| **4** 6225 | **14** climb |
| **5** ROOM | **15** earth |
| **6** spin | **16** FLAT FLAN |
| **7** then | **17** BUST BEST |
| **8** inch | **18** CART CARD |
| **9** drop | **19** CORN BORN |
| **10** reel or sate | **20** FLEW BLEW |

## TEST 14: **Mixed**

| | |
|---|---|
| **1** sharks  dwell | **12** more, got |
| **2** seventy thirty | **13** snow, dark |
| **3** rugby football | **14** shirt, favourite |
| **4** homeless streets | **15** Saturdays, football |
| **5** ostrich | **16** BROAD |
| **6** forwards | **17** BROTH |
| **7** breakfast | **18–20** |
| **8** afternoon | |
| **9** matchstick | |
| **10** waterfall | |
| **11** quietly, door | |

| S | I | D | E | S |
|---|---|---|---|---|
| A | | R | | U |
| F | L | I | N | G |
| E | | E | | A |
| R | A | R | E | R |

## TEST 15: **Mixed**

**1** kicked, ball, back
**2** man, newspaper, read
**3** How, you, books
**4** clock, chimes, twelve
**5** write, sharpen, pencil

| | |
|---|---|
| **6** stick | |
| **7** treat | **14** HEIGHT |
| **8** unless | **15** TIGER |
| **9** stride | **16** 32 26 |
| **10** please | **17** 35 42 |
| **11** 7612 | **18** 8 64 |
| **12** 26153 | **19** 7 20 |
| **13** HERB | **20** 55 19 |

## TEST 16: **Mixed**

**1–3**

| C | H | A | S | M |
|---|---|---|---|---|
| H | | W | O | T |
| A | W | A | I | T |
| I | | R | O | |
| R | A | D | A | R |

**4–6**

| S | O | C | K | S |
|---|---|---|---|---|
| T | | R | | H |
| O | L | I | V | E |
| R | | M | | D |
| M | E | E | T | S |

**7** B  **9** MFBG
**8** SPX  **10** SUNNY

## TEST 17: **Mixed**

**1–4** A Ford, Vauxhall
B metre, millimetre
C Berlin, Venice
D pineapple, banana

| | |
|---|---|
| **5** CREASE | **13** TOAST |
| **6** PALATE | **14** STALE |
| **7** DREAD | **15** SPARE |
| **8** TAMPER | **16** PLASTER |
| **9** circle, box | **17** crown wig |
| **10** cup or plate | **18** scales feathers |
| **11** finger, shoe | **19** pork  beef |
| **12** tooth, lip | **20** nail  nut |

**11** PEAR STEAK  **15** TIED TROUT
**12** MANE HUGE  **16** star
**13** FAIL STRAY  **17** tile
**14** ROOM BLED  **18** iron
  **19** wall
  **20** bust

## TEST 18: **Mixed**

| | |
|---|---|
| **1** check | B=beans |
| **2** well | C=carrots |
| **3** reflect | D= mushrooms |
| **4** limit | E= tomatoes |
| **5** cheap | |
| **6** SUX | **16** ICED |
| **7** QO | **17** FLEX |
| **8** TG | **18** LAMB |
| **9** HE | **19** GATE |
| **10** SpV | **20** PLUG |
| **11–15** A= cucumber | |

## TEST 19: **Mixed**

| | |
|---|---|
| **1** off, on | **11** r |
| **2** warm, cool | **12** e |
| **3** for, against | **13** k |
| **4** give, take | **14** y |
| **5** sharp, blunt | **15** d |
| **6** UW  YA | **16** 9471 |
| **7** UU  TV | **17** 9413 |
| **8** HFI  IGJ | **18** 9331 |
| **9** KP  MN | **19** 7413 |
| **10** kjl  lkm | **20** KALE |

## TEST 20: **Mixed**

| | |
|---|---|
| **1** sawn | **11** ?/+£* |
| **2** stun | **12** write, paint |
| **3** bran | **13** milk, carton |
| **4** rein | **14** Top, low |
| **5** pill | **15** think, digest |
| **6** B | **16** stop, red |
| **7** COST | **17** 4 |
| **8** SCHOOL | **18** 6 |
| **9** CHEESE | **19** 12 |
| **10** /+?*! | **20** 7 |

## TEST 21: **Mixed**

| | |
|---|---|
| **1** fence | **11** harpoon |
| **2** sauce | **12** largesse |
| **3** muddle | **13** EEL |
| **4** slice | **14** AIR |
| **5** water | **15** AND |
| **6** fire | **16** HER |
| **7** snow | **17** PI  SF |
| **8** rain | **18** GF  IH |
| **9** flatworm | **19** LS  MT |
| **10** stagnant | **20** DR  EQ |

## TEST 22: **Mixed**

| | |
|---|---|
| **1** win, lose | **13** cane, bred |
| **2** warm, cool | **14** light, carp |
| **3** clear, cloudy | **15** sue, turn |
| **4** collect, deliver | **16** food, hilt |
| **5** 11 | **17** SHAPES, PHASES |
| **6** 10 | |
| **7** 5 | **18** GRUNTS, STRUNG |
| **8** 6 | |
| **9** dart | **19** STAPLE, PALEST |
| **10** fair | |
| **11** eject | **20** STALE, LEAST |
| **12** stout | |

## TEST 23: **Mixed**

**1–5**
B A E E C
D A B D C

| | |
|---|---|
| **6** FAME | **13** empty |
| **7** HEAT | **14** uneven |
| **8** PLAN | **15** noisy |
| **9** CATER | **16** climb, ascend |
| **10** ADDER | **17** concur, agree |
| **11** thick | **18** healthy, well |
| **12** difficult | **19** arrow, dart |
| | **20** carpet, rug |

## Test 24: Mixed

1 library, bank
2 weekend, weekday
3 bite, peck
4 pip, stone
5 boat, bicycle
6 GAME SAME
7 PLAY PRAY
8 SITE MITE
9 BASH BATH
10 FORK FORT
11 spaceship
12 roadworks
13 honeycomb
14 bullseye
15 headlong
16 11
17 soft
18 7
19 5
20 16

## Test 25: Mixed

1 headstrong, stubborn
2 border, edge
3 edgy, tense
4 mutiny, revolt
5 power, strength
6 music, radio
7 spoke, telephone
8 leave, books, teacher
9 hippo, rivers, mouth
10 brushes, morning, flannel
11 DM HQ
12 GT LO
13 GS HQ
14 515 533
15 10 23
16 26 28
17 land
18 wild
19 high
20 wind

## Test 26: Mixed

1 s
2 b
3 n
4 p
5 e

6–8

| P | I | E | C | E |
| R |   | D |   | A |
| E | A | G | E | R |
| E |   | E |   | L |
| N | O | S | E | Y |

9–11

| F | L | A | S | H |
| I |   | N |   | O |
| R | I | G | H | T |
| E |   | L |   | E |
| S | T | E | A | L |

12 put, where
13 morning, get
14 pavilion, ball
15 table, book
16 hero
17 hall
18 rest
19 tall
20 here

## Test 27: Mixed

1 October
2 December
3 March
4 ODMBHK
5 BQZXNM
6 SPOONS
7 PLATES
8 26 31
9 11 8
10 16 64
11 20 5
12 touch, feel
13 nail, tack
14 oar, paddle
15 teacher, instructor

16 blackberry
17 armchair
18 roundabout
19 pillowcase
20 hedgerow

## Test 28: Mixed

1 fair
2 right
3 plain
4 rich
5 9
6 10
7 6
8 8
9 shot
10 mean
11 test
12 tilt
13 OUR
14 EAR
15 TEA
16 TEN
17 swallow
18 teacher
19 cross
20 noise

## Test 29: Mixed

1 al
2 le
3 fe
4 th
5 PINES
6 PLEAT
7 CLASP
8 TRUST

9–12 A Brian, Susan
B bus, train
C squash, beer
D for, under

13 azure
14 tranquil
15 weep
16 bristle
17 8
18 12
19 10
20 13

## Test 30: Mixed

1 tennis, racquet, court
2 goldfish, swam, pond-weed
3 weather, rainy, ground
4 Mum
5 Sarah
6 Tom
7 Pete
8 Dad
9 grief
10 cute
11 shake
12 pride
13 trend
14 gush
15 9064
16 9884
17 0643
18 9480
19 TOWN
20 ANTS

## Test 31: Mixed

1 PEAR
2 STOP
3 KING
4 TEAL
5 SPUR
6 complete, start
7 expose, conceal
8 distant, approachable
9 genuine, fake
10 praise, criticise
11 D
12 8
13 2
14 5
15 31
16 ACILPST
17 ACEMPRS
18 ADEIMNRSU
19 ABDEKORY
20 E

## Test 32: Mixed

1 f
2 g
3 n
4 w
5 evening, morning
6 navy, ruby
7 broth, belief
8 drop, lower
9 WALL WILL
10 TRAP TRIP
11 LIFE LIME
12 SHOT SOOT
13 homework
14 eggshell
15 backwards
16 grandstand
17 ankle
18 look
19 London
20 Instruct

## Test 33: Mixed

1 EASEL, LEASE
2 THROW, WORTH
3 SPORE, PROSE
4 U\W
5 P70
6 v37X
7 YxW
8 SR
9 T–W
10 bed
11 black
12 life
13 some
14 hard, banks, road
15 bed, pyjamas, hair
16 cinema, hurry, film
17 i
18 m
19 j
20 n

## Test 34: Mixed

1 OPQ WXY
2 37 33
3 G24 O48
4 10 15
5 strong
6 interior
7 coach
8 interest
9 listen
10 plain
11 tracing
12 stammer
13 AND
14 OAT
15 HAM
16 NET
17 c
18 p
19 n
20 o

## Test 35: Mixed

1 ASLEEP
2 PRIEST
3 TRELLIS
4 SPADES
5 STREAM
6 SHEARS
7 SHALLOW
8 BELLOW
9 crow, clock
10 rubber, ruler
11 classroom, teacher
12 cube, pyramid
13 four, three
14 scales, fur
15 lid, roof
16 drive, beach
17 efface
18 added
19 faced
20 dead

## Test 36: Mixed

1 ?!%/\
2 £:/*!
3 STRICT
4 ASSIST
5 3 1 2 12 5
6 6 1 3 5 4

**7–9**

| C | L | A | | M | S |
|---|---|---|---|---|---|
| R | | L | | | T |
| A | R | M | O | U | R |
| D | | O | | O | |
| L | | N | | N | |
| E | N | D | I | N | G |

**10–12**

| B | U | S | T | L | E |
|---|---|---|---|---|---|
| O | | U | | A | |
| U | D | D | E | R | S |
| N | | D | | G | |
| D | E | E | P | E | R |
| | S | | N | | R |

13 your
14 rent
15 stem
16 done
17 Bourne
18 Dalton
19 south
20 south-east

## Test 37: Mixed

1 PLAY
  SLAY
2 TYRE
  TORE
3 CLOP
  CROP
4 FOUL
  FOOL
5 b
6 l
7 a
8 g
9 MN
10 UWZ
11 caterpillar, leaf
12 fast, hare
13 l28
14 ;/$@
15 gun, bullet
16 time, clock
17 guinea-pigs, Sally
18 salad, chicken
19 maths, finding
20 starts, television

## Test 38: Mixed

1 plate
2 plant
3 rout
4 bug
5 blown
6 narrow
7 over
8 speak
9 illuminate
10 fasten
11 40 24
12 11, 10
13 t18 v31
14 GIT HJS
15 EHf CFd
16 MOAT
17 DRIP
18 RAID
19 TAIL
20 DEAL

## Test 39: Mixed

1 Fern
2 Naomi
3 Husna
4 Debra
5 Naomi
6 NKIJV
7 FCTMPGUU
8 LUCKY
9 CRAZY
10 rigid, sturdy
11 defeat, conquer
12 inaccurate, false
13 firm, harsh
14 proud, arrogant
15 A D G H R T U
16 C E M O P R T U
17 DRAWL, DRAWN, DREAM
18 HEARTH HEARTY HEATER
19 Saturday
20 R

## Test 40: Mixed

1 12 12
2 ZAB YBC
3 15b 11a
4 RSq ZAy
5 WORD WARD
6 ROSE RISE
7 LAZE LAME
8 RICE RISE
9 PURE SURE
10 BEAT BOAT
11 FLEA FLEW
12 HOME HOSE
13 w
14 h
15 p
16 e

**17–20**
1C=Clement
1D=Pravin
2F=Kang
2G=Harold
2J=Gretel
3E=Penelope
4D=Sandra
4E=Judy

## Puzzle ❷

1 PARK PACK SACK
2 BELT BEST BUST
3 MOAN MOON MOOR
4 PINT MINT MIST
5 CROW BROW BLOW

## Puzzle ❸

| | RELATIVE | TREAT |
|---|---|---|
| Lucy | grandpa | donkey ride |
| Clare | aunt | ice cream |
| James | sister | funfair |
| Jamila | mum | beach games |

## Puzzle ❶

**1**

| P | R | I | Z | E |
|---|---|---|---|---|
| R | | N | | N |
| I | N | L | E | T |
| Z | | E | | E |
| E | N | T | E | R |

**2**

| A | W | A | R | E |
|---|---|---|---|---|
| W | | C | | N |
| A | C | R | I | D |
| R | | I | | E |
| E | N | D | E | D |

**3**

| S | A | | T | S |
|---|---|---|---|---|
| A | | I | | T |
| L | I | V | E | R |
| T | | E | | A |
| S | | R | A | P |

**4**

| B | A | T | O | N |
|---|---|---|---|---|
| A | | A | | E |
| T | A | U | P | E |
| O | | P | | D |
| N | E | E | D | S |

**5**

| M | E | A | T |
|---|---|---|---|
| E | A | C | H |
| A | C | H | E |
| T | H | E | N |

**6**

| D | A | I | S |
|---|---|---|---|
| A | U | N | T |
| I | N | T | O |
| S | T | O | P |

**7**

| P | R | A | Y |
|---|---|---|---|
| R | A | R | E |
| A | R | E | A |
| Y | E | A | R |

**8**

| S | I | G | N |
|---|---|---|---|
| I | D | E | A |
| G | E | R | M |
| N | A | M | E |

**9**

| E | A | G | E | R |
|---|---|---|---|---|
| A | L | O | N | E |
| G | O | U | D | A |
| E | N | D | E | D |
| R | E | A | D | S |

**10**

| S | T | A | M | P |
|---|---|---|---|---|
| T | H | R | E | E |
| A | R | E | A | S |
| M | E | A | N | T |
| P | E | S | T | O |

## Puzzle ❹

1 water
2 eating
3 sentence

## Puzzle ❺

Possible answers include:

**6-letter**
staple, pastel, petals, plates, pleats, palest

**5-letter**
stale, steal, tales, plate, pleas, slept, pleat, least, pelts, slate, splat, lapse, petal, pales

**4-letter**
last, salt, plea, slap, slat, pale, sale, late, tale, leap, seal, peal, pelt, lets, leas

**3-letter**
let, lap, pal, ale, lea

Test time: 0    5    10 minutes

Complete the following sentences in the best way by choosing one word from each set of brackets.

**Example**  Tall is to (tree, short, colour) as narrow is to (thin, white, wide).

**1**  Book is to (library, author, paper) as money is to (cash, bank, exchange).

**2**  Saturday is to (weekend, supermarket, holiday) as Monday is to (washing, weekday, school).

**3**  Tooth is to (bite, filling, mouth) as beak is to (nest, worms, peck).

**4**  Apple is to (wine, juice, pip) as peach is to (apricot, stone, tree).

**5**  Oar is to (mine, ship, boat) as pedal is to (bicycle, horse, pushers).

Change the first word into the last word by changing one letter at a time, and making two new, different words in the middle.

**Example**  CASE  _CASH_  _WASH_  WISH

**6**  GATE  _____  _____  SOME  **7**  PLAN  _____  _____  PREY

**8**  SIZE  _____  _____  MUTE  **9**  BASK  _____  _____  BOTH

**10**  WORK  _____  _____  FONT

Underline two words, one from each group, that go together to form a new word. The word in the first group always comes first.

**Example**  (hand, green, for)   (light, house, sure)

**11**  (old, space, fishing) (age, ship, boat)  **12**  (road, lane, street)  (works, stop, gear)

**13**  (darling, honey, hare) (brush, hive, comb)  **14**  (pigs, bulls, birds)  (eye, ear, nose)

**15**  (bread, stick, head) (short, long, wide)

From the information supplied, answer the questions.

There were 23 different types of cheese on a cheese counter at the farm shop.
There were four different types of soft goats' cheese, two of these were Welsh, the rest English.
There were seven other types of soft cheese; five cows' cheeses and two cheeses made from milk taken from sheep. All these were English.
There were 12 hard cows' cheeses, three from Wales and two from Ireland.

**16**  How many soft cheeses were there?  _____

**17**  Are the sheep's cheeses soft or hard?  _____

**18**  How many English hard cheeses were there?  _____

**19**  How many Welsh cheeses were there altogether?  _____

**20**  How many English cheeses were there altogether?  _____

25

*Time for a break! Go to Puzzle Page 44* ▶

Total  _____

Test time: 0 | | | | | 5 | | | | | 10 minutes

Underline the two words, one from each group, that are closest in meaning.

**Example** (race, shop, <u>start</u>)     (finish, <u>begin</u>, end)

1   (headlong, headstrong, headline)   (stubborn, lengthy, mark)
2   (clothes, line, border)   (flower, straight, edge)
3   (edgy, calm, sensible)   (tender, tense, hectic)
4   (pirate, mutiny, crew)   (revolt, repulse, revive)
5   (power, tower, mower)   (length, width, strength)

Complete the following sentences by selecting the most sensible word from each group of words given in the brackets. Underline the words selected.

**Example**   The (<u>children</u>, boxes, foxes) carried the (houses, <u>books</u>, steps) home from the (greengrocer, <u>library</u>, factory).

6   My aunt listens to (music, tortoises, trees) on the (bathroom, radio, dustbin).
7   I (spoke, saw, ran) to Jo on the (television, park, telephone).
8   "Kindly (eat, leave, climb) those (tomatoes, stairs, books) alone!" shouted the (desk, teacher, goldfish).
9   A (hippo, giraffe, mouse) lives mostly in African (rivers, houses, airports) and has a big (ear, mouth, neck).
10   Before Adam (combs, counts, brushes) his teeth in the (classroom, morning, jungle) he likes to wash his face with his (flannel, hairbrush, dog).

A B C D E F G H I J K L M N O P Q R S T U V W X Y Z

Give the two missing groups of letters or numbers in the following sequences. The alphabet has been written out to help you.

**Example**   CQ   DP   EQ   FP   <u>*GQ*</u>   <u>*HP*</u>

| 11 | CL | ___ | EN | FO | GP | ___ | **12** | ___ | HS | IR | JQ | KP | ___ |
|----|----|-----|----|----|----|-----|--------|-----|----|----|----|----|-----|
| **13** | FY | FW | GU | ___ | ___ | HO | **14** | 506 | ___ | 524 | ___ | 542 | 551 |
| **15** | 17 | ___ | 20 | 20 | ___ | 30 | 26 | 40 | | | | | |
| **16** | 24 | 25 | ___ | 26 | 28 | 27 | 30 | ___ | | | | | |

Find a word that can be put in front of each of the following words to make a new, compound word.

**Example**   cast    fall    ward    pour    <u>*down*</u>

| 17 | owner | fill | lady | mark | _____ |
|----|-------|------|------|------|-----------|
| 18 | life | cat | fowl | fire | _____ |
| 19 | ness | lighter | light | land | _____ |
| 20 | swept | surfing | screen | pipe | _____ |

Total

Test time: 0     5     10 minutes

Find the letter which will end the first word and start the second word.

**Example**   peac ( h ) ome

**1**   las (__) oak          **2**   gru (__) ook          **3**   ru (__) ewt

**4**   cram (__) ole        **5**   kit (__) lse

Fill in the crosswords so that all the words are included.

**6–8**

EARLY   NOSEY

EAGER   PREEN

PIECE   EDGES

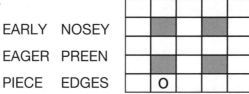

**9–11**

STEAL   FLASH

HOTEL   FIRES

ANGLE   RIGHT

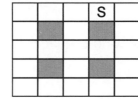

Find and underline the two words that need to change places for each sentence to make sense.

**Example**   She went to <u>letter</u> the <u>write</u>.

**12**   Put did you where the car keys?

**13**   Sam promised to morning up early in the get.

**14**   The batsman hit the pavilion over the ball.

**15**   He found a table he really liked on a book.

Write the four-letter word hidden at the end of one word and the beginning of the next word. The order of the letters may not be changed.

**Example**   We had bat<u>s and</u> balls.                              _sand_

**16**   My uncle says you must take the rough with the smooth.   _____

**17**   The teacher was very angry with all the class.   _____

**18**   Mrs Blewitt says they are stored in her greenhouse.   _____

**19**   Mandy has gone to collect all the hockey balls.   _____

**20**   A young swallow has migrated with the rest of the birds.   _____

Total

If the months were put in alphabetical order, which would be:

**1** the second last month? _____

**2** the third month? _____

**3** the month after June? _____

A B C D E F G H I J K L M N O P Q R S T U V W X Y Z

The word BOTTLE is written in code as ANSSKD. Encode each of these words using the same code.

**4** PENCIL _____ **5** CRAYON _____

Decode these words using the same code as above.

**6** RONNMR _____ **7** OKZSDR _____

Give the two missing numbers in the following sequences.

**Example** CQ DP EQ FP _GQ_ _HP_

| **8** | ____ | ____ | 36 | 41 | 46 | 51 | | |
|---|---|---|---|---|---|---|---|---|
| **9** | 5 | 9 | 6 | 10 | 7 | ____ | ____ | |
| **10** | 4 | 8 | ____ | 32 | ____ | 128 | | |
| **11** | 16 | 9 | 18 | 7 | ____ | ____ | 22 | 3 |

Underline two words from the group which are most similar in type or meaning.

**Example** <u>dear</u> pleasant poor extravagant <u>expensive</u>

| **12** | touch | feel | smoke | laugh | ring |
|---|---|---|---|---|---|
| **13** | hammer | nail | finger | tack | varnish |
| **14** | coal | gem | oar | majesty | paddle |
| **15** | neighbour | teacher | friend | niece | instructor |

Underline two words, one from each group, that go together to form a new word. The word in the first group always comes first.

**Example** (hand, <u>green</u>, for) (light, <u>house</u>, sure)

| **16** | (sea, green, black) | (berry, current, piece) |
|---|---|---|
| **17** | (turn, right, arm) | (gate, stop, chair) |
| **18** | (ground, round, water) | (under, about, place) |
| **19** | (pillow, briefs, picnic) | (place, case, sheet) |
| **20** | (vegetable, grass, hedge) | (wood, green, row) |

Total

Underline one word in brackets that will go equally well with both pairs of words outside the brackets.

**Example** rush, attack      cost, fee          (price, hasten, strike, <u>charge</u>, money)

**1**    just, equal          blonde, light        (fair, plus, yellow, appropriate, true)

**2**    correct, precise      fix, mend            (exact, wrong, right, sum, sort)

**3**    undecorated, simple   clear, direct         (easy, ugly, flat, plain, straight)

**4**    wealthy, affluent      unhealthy, creamy    (satisfactory, well, rich, correctly, strong)

If a = 2, b = 5, c = 4, d = 3 and e = 10, find the value of the following.

**5**   $d + a + c = $ _____     **6**   $\dfrac{e}{a} + b = $ _____     **7**   $\dfrac{de}{b} = $ _____     **8**   $(e - d) + (b - c) = $ _____

Write the four-letter word hidden at the end of one word and the beginning of the next word. The order of the letters may not be changed.

**Example** We had bat<u>s and</u> balls.                  _____*sand*_____

**9**    If you push other people out of the way, you will be punished.    _____

**10**   Ruby's new bike had a black frame and a white saddle.         _____

**11**   It takes forty minutes to cook my lasagne.                _____

**12**   She counted the hours until the bell rang.                _____

Find the three-letter word that can be added to the letters in capitals to make a new word. The new word will complete the sentence sensibly. Write the three-letter word.

**Example** The cat sprang onto the MO.         _____USE_____

**13**   The JNEY to Scotland took a long time.        _____

**14**   The old man had a long grey BD.              _____

**15**   Don't burn yourself on the SM from the kettle.   _____

**16**   The BEA finalist congratulated the winner.     _____

Underline the one word in each group that **cannot be made** from the letters of the word in capital letters.

**Example** STATIONERY    stone      tyres       ration      <u>nation</u>      noisy

**17**   PILLOWCASE    swallow    lapse      scalp       callow      scale

**18**   CHARACTER     crater     charter    earth       teacher     reach

**19**   CHROMOSOME   choose    morose    chrome    rooms       cross

**20**   TRANSITION     artist      nations    noise       strait      station

Total

Find two letters that will end the first word and start the second word.

**Example**  pas ( t̲  a̲ ) ste

**1**  pet (__ __) ter       **2**  hand (__ __) dge

**3**  kni (__ __) arless       **4**  mou (__ __) orn

Rearrange the letters in capitals to make another word. The new word has something to do with the first two words or phrases.

**Example**  spot    soil    SAINT    STAIN

| | | | | |
|---|---|---|---|---|
| **5** | longs for | yearns | SNIPE | _____ |
| **6** | fold | crease | PETAL | _____ |
| **7** | clutch | pin part of a brooch | SCALP | _____ |
| **8** | faith | belief | STRUT | _____ |

Look at these words. Sort them into groups.

**9–12**  Brian    bus    for    train    under    squash    Susan    beer

| A Names | B Transport | C Drinks | D Prepositions |
|---|---|---|---|
| _____ | _____ | _____ | _____ |
| _____ | _____ | _____ | _____ |

Underline the word in brackets closest in meaning to the word in capitals.

**Example**  UNHAPPY    (unkind, death, laughter, sad, friendly)

**13**  BLUE  (pink, bruise, sky, downfall, azure)    **14**  CALM  (lake, rough, kind, tranquil, stormy)

**15**  CRY  (whisper, weep, call, say, tearful)    **16**  STUBBLE  (chin, field, straw, bristle, fall)

From the information supplied, complete the statements.

I was 4 when my brother was born. My father was 8 times older than I was then.

**17**  When my father is 40 my brother will be _____ years old.

**18**  When I am 16, my brother will be _____ years old.

From the information supplied, answer the questions.

Z is a number. Double it and take away 2. Divide by 3 and the answer is 6.

**19**  What is Z?  _____

**20**  What would Z be if you take away 8 instead of 2?  _____

Total

Complete the following sentences by selecting the most sensible word from each group of words given in the brackets. Underline the words selected.

**Example** The (<u>children</u>, boxes, foxes) carried the (houses, <u>books</u>, steps) home from the (greengrocer, <u>library</u>, factory).

**1** The (tennis, football, golf) player lifted his (club, racquet, shirt) and hit the ball into the (yard, goal, court).

**2** The (banana, goldfish, man) (swam, climbed, lay) around the bowl amongst the (pondweed, kitchen, salad).

**3** The weather forecaster said the (rain, weather, cloud) would be (weather, rainy, map) this afternoon with snow on high (ground, tea, cloud).

From the information supplied, answer the questions.

A family went to the swimming baths and put their clothes in different lockers.
Mum, Sarah and Tom put their clothes in lockers next door to each other.
Pete put his in the locker opposite Tom's. Dad and Sarah used even numbered lockers.
The unavailable lockers are shaded. Who used which locker?

**4** Locker 3 _____

**5** Locker 4 _____

**6** Locker 5 _____

**7** Locker 12 _____

**8** Locker 14 _____

| 1 | 2 | 3 | 4 | 5 | 6 | 7 |
|---|---|---|---|---|---|---|
| 8 | 9 | 10 | 11 | 12 | 13 | 14 |

Find a word that is similar in meaning to the word in capital letters and that rhymes with the second word.

**Example** CABLE   tyre   *wire*

**9** MISERY   beef   _____

**10** PRETTY   suit   _____

**11** QUIVER   brake   _____

**12** CONCEIT   wide   _____

**13** FASHION   friend   _____

**14** POUR   thrush   _____

Here are the number codes for four words.
9480   0643   9064   9884
Match the right code to the right word.

**15** SWAN _____   **16** SOON _____   **17** WANT_____   **18** SNOW _____

Decode these words using the same code as above.

**19** 3804 _____      **20** 6439 _____

Total

Look at the first group of three words. The word in the middle has been made from the two other words. Complete the second group of three words in the same way, making a new word in the middle of the group.

**Example** PA<u>IN</u>  INTO  <u>TO</u>OK     ALSO   <u>SOON</u>   ONLY

| 1 | SIZE | ZEST | STUN | TYPE | _____ | ARCH |
| 2 | TRIP | PILL | TELL | FATS | _____ | DROP |
| 3 | SEER | REED | ENDS | WICK | _____ | NAGS |
| 4 | EBBS | SEEN | NEWT | EMIT | _____ | LAMB |
| 5 | FEUD | DUET | TRAM | CUPS | _____ | ROUT |

Underline the two words, one from each group, which are the most opposite in meaning.

**Example**  (dawn, <u>early</u>, wake)     (<u>late</u>, stop, sunrise)

| 6 | (complete, compete, compel) | (entire, start, win) |
| 7 | (hide, expose, cruise) | (depose, conceal, decrease) |
| 8 | (stately, friendly, distant) | (approachable, anger, dislike) |
| 9 | (dead, genuine, alive) | (real, blunt, fake) |
| 10 | (praise, practise, prance) | (criticise, compliment, commend) |

From the information supplied, underline the one statement below it that must be true.

**11**   Sheena was given a pot plant. It was not watered so it died.

    **A** The plant was a birthday present.     **C** Sheena liked plants.

    **B** Sheena was too busy to water the plant.     **D** The plant needed water to stay alive.

If a = 10, b = 4, c = 3 and d = 5, find the value of the following.

**12**   $\dfrac{ab}{d}$ = ___    **13**   (b + c) − (a − d) = ___    **14**   $\dfrac{bd}{a}$ + c = ___    **15**   (b − c) + ac = ___

Write the letters in the following words in alphabetical order.

**16**   PLASTIC    _____     **17**   SCAMPER    _____

**18**   NURSEMAID    _____     **19**   KEYBOARD    _____

From the information supplied answer the question.

I appear twice in INNUMERABLE, once in SINCE and not at all in NATIONAL.

**20**   Which letter is being described? ____

Total

Find the one letter that will end the first word and start the second word of each pair of words. The same letter must be used for both pairs of words.

**Example** mea ( t ) able    fi ( t ) ab

| | | | |
|---|---|---|---|
| **1** | staf (___) oxes    clif (___) ades | **2** | sta (___) lue    fro (___) reet |
| **3** | trai (___) ight    toxi (___) ails | **4** | ja (___) ail    stra (___) hen |

Complete the following sentences in the best way by choosing one word from each set of brackets.

**Example** Tall is to (tree, <u>short</u>, colour) as narrow is to (thin, white, <u>wide</u>).

**5** Dusk is to (sunset, evening, dark) as dawn is to (beginning, hours, morning).

**6** Blue is to (sky, black, navy) as red is to (orange, blood, ruby).

**7** Fact is to (truth, guess, idea) as opinion is to (proof, evidence, belief).

**8** Fall is to (drop, water, autumn) as descend is to (lower, raise, winter).

Change the first word into the last word by changing one letter at a time, and making two new, different words in the middle.

**Example** CASE  _CASH_   _WASH_   WISH

| | | | | | | |
|---|---|---|---|---|---|---|
| **9** | WALK | _____ _____ | PILL | **10** | TRAY _____ _____ | DRIP |
| **11** | LIFT | _____ _____ | LAME | **12** | SHOE _____ _____ | BOOT |

Underline two words, one from each group, that go together to form a new word. The word in the first group always comes first.

**Example** (hand, <u>green</u>, for)   (light, <u>house</u>, sure)

**13** (home, guest, hotel)   (going, work, bill)

**14** (yolk, egg, soup)   (plate, pudding, shell)

**15** (back, drake, lever)   (let, wards, for)

**16** (low, high, grand)   (sit, stand, seat)

Underline the word in the brackets which goes best with the words given outside the brackets.

**Example** word, paragraph, sentence       (pen, cap, <u>letter</u>, top, stop)

**17** elbow, shoulder, knee       (leg, arm, ankle, head, body)

**18** peek, glance, peep       (mountain, sight, stare, eyes, look)

**19** Belfast, Edinburgh, Cardiff   (Athens, Dublin, England, London, Iceland)

**20** coach, train, drill       (engine, instruct, tool, man, rails)

( 33 )

Total [____]

# TEST 33: **Mixed**

Underline the two words that are made from the same letters.

**Example** TAP   PET   <u>TEA</u>   POT   <u>EAT</u>

| | | | | |
|---|---|---|---|---|
| **1** EASEL | LEAST | SLATS | LEASE | STEEL |
| **2** WORST | WRATH | THROW | WORTH | THREW |
| **3** RASPS | SPORE | SPARE | PROSE | SPOON |

A B C D E F G H I J K L M N O P Q R S T U V W X Y Z

Fill in the missing letters, symbols or numbers.

**Example** AB is to CD as PQ is to __RS__ .

**4** A/C is to E\G as Q/S is to _____.

**5** G25 is to H30 as O65 is to _____.

**6** f14H is to j20L as r31T is to _____.

**7** HgF is to EdC as BaZ is to _____.

**8** LK is to HG as WV is to _____.

**9** M+P is to S – V as N+Q is to _____.

Find a word that can be put in front of each of the following words to make a new, compound word.

**Example** cast   fall   ward   pour   __down__

**10** time   clothes   room   spread   _____

**11** board   list   mail   bird   _____

**12** time   long   blood   less   _____

**13** thing   one   where   what   _____

Complete the following sentences by selecting the most sensible word from each group of words given in the brackets. Underline the words selected.

**Example** The (<u>children</u>, boxes, foxes) carried the (houses, <u>books</u>, steps) home from the (greengrocer, <u>library</u>, factory).

**14** It was raining so (soft, slowly, hard) that the river burst its (banks, balloons, beds) and flooded the (crowd, road, river).

**15** Before going to (school, church, bed) at night, Tracey puts on her (pyjamas, anorak, skis) and brushes her (shoes, carpets, hair).

**16** We arrived late at the (cinema, ferry, shop) so had to (eat, rest, hurry) to see the beginning of the (book, film, concert).

If i = 10, j = 12, k = 4, l = 5, m = 3 and n = 2, find the value of the following. Write your answers as letters.

**17** $\dfrac{jl}{i} + k =$ _____

**18** $(i + m + n) - j =$ _____

**19** $k^2 - n^2 =$ _____

**20** $\dfrac{j}{m} - \dfrac{i}{l} =$ _____

Total

Test time: 0    5    10 minutes

A B C D E F G H I J K L M N O P Q R S T U V W X Y Z

Give the two missing groups of letters and numbers in the following sequences.
The alphabet has been written out to help you.

**Example**  CQ   DP   EQ   FP   _GQ_   _HP_

| | | | | | | | | |
|---|---|---|---|---|---|---|---|---|
| **1** | GHI | KLM | ____ | STU | ____ | ABC | | |
| **2** | 66 | 17 | 55 | 27 | 44 | ____ | ____ | 47 |
| **3** | a6 | C12 | e18 | ____ | i30 | K36 | m42 | ____ |
| **4** | 3 | 6 | ____ | ____ | 21 | 28 | 36 | 45 |

Underline one word in brackets that will go equally well with both pairs of words outside the brackets.

**Example**  rush, attack     cost, fee        (price, hasten, strike, <u>charge</u>, money)

| | | | |
|---|---|---|---|
| **5** | muscular, powerful | solid, stable | (frozen, strong, long-lasting, consistent, melted) |
| **6** | inner, inside | centre, core | (interior, inland, exterior, indoors, island) |
| **7** | instructor, tutor | teach, drill | (scout, bus, coach, student, learn) |
| **8** | hobby, activity | attention, curiosity | (interview, interfere, interest, intercept, intern) |

Underline the one word in each group that **can be made** from the letters of the word in capital letters.

**Example**  CHAMPION      camping     notch      peach      cramp      <u>chimp</u>

| | | | | | | |
|---|---|---|---|---|---|---|
| **9** | NESTLING | guest | slings | stink | gentle | listen |
| **10** | PINEAPPLE | ample | pliant | plain | planet | ripple |
| **11** | SCRATCHING | grate | tracing | strings | crouch | search |
| **12** | MAINSTREAM | straits | stammer | monster | strains | matter |

Find the three-letter word that can be added to the letters in capitals to make a new word. The new word will complete the sentence sensibly. Write the three-letter word.

**Example**  The cat sprang onto the MO.          _USE_

| | | |
|---|---|---|
| **13** | The door HLE has broken. | _____ |
| **14** | We have lots of GS on our farm. | _____ |
| **15** | The bottle of SPOO is in the bathroom. | _____ |
| **16** | Some metals are MAGIC. | _____ |

Which one letter can be added to the front of all of these words to make new words?

**Example**  _C_are   _C_at   _C_rate   _C_all   _C_lip

**17**  __ash   __art   __hart   __hair   __lap   **18**  __arched   __ill   __inch   __rim   __ale

**19**  __arrow   __early   __either   __eat   __ail   **20**  __pen   __pal   __wing   __range   __at

Total

Rearrange the letters in capitals to make another word. The new word has something to do with the first two words or phrases.

| Example | spot | soil | SAINT | *STAIN* |
|---------|------|------|-------|---------|
| 1 | inattentive | not awake | PLEASE | _____ |
| 2 | preacher | holy man | STRIPE | _____ |
| 3 | framework | support for plants | TILLERS | _____ |
| 4 | suit in cards | digging tools | PASSED | _____ |

Add one letter to the word in capital letters to make a new word. The meaning of the new word is given in the clue.

| Example | PLAN | simple | *PLAIN* |
|---------|------|--------|---------|
| 5 | STEAM | a small river | _____ |
| 6 | HEARS | a cutting tool | _____ |
| 7 | SALLOW | not deep | _____ |
| 8 | BELOW | to shout | _____ |

Underline the two words that are the odd ones out in each group of words.

Example  black  <u>king</u>  purple  green  <u>house</u>

| 9 | scare | crow | fright | shock | clock |
|----|-------|------|--------|-------|-------|
| 10 | pencil | rubber | ruler | pen | biro |
| 11 | history | geography | biology | classroom | teacher |
| 12 | cube | triangle | square | pyramid | rectangle |

Complete the following sentences in the best way by choosing one word from each set of brackets.

Example  Tall is to (tree, <u>short</u>, colour) as narrow is to (thin, white, <u>wide</u>).

13  Chair is to (four, six, two) as stool is to (kitchen, three, legs).

14  Fish is to (water, fin, scales) as bear is to (cub, fur, honey).

15  Box is to (cardboard, lid, label) as house is to (roof, chimney, upstairs).

16  Gravel is to (drive, stone, grey) as sand is to (castle, beach, Blackpool).

Underline any words below that contain only the first six letters of the alphabet.

| 17 | coffee | beach | efface | dabble | dance |
|----|--------|-------|--------|--------|-------|
| 18 | pebble | back | clubs | basin | added |
| 19 | fiction | freckle | fatigue | fudge | faced |
| 20 | abacus | dead | dread | cradle | adding |

Total

The code for the word CHRISTMAS is *!/%?\£:?. Encode each of these words using the same code.

**1** SHIRT _____

**2** MARCH _____

Decode these words using the same code as above.

**3** ?\/%*\ _____

**4** :??%?\ _____

The code for the word DABBLE is 4 1 2 2 12 5. Encode each of these words using the same code.

**5** CABLE _____

**6** FACED _____

Fill in the crosswords so that all the words are included.

**7–9**

| | | | | | |
|---|---|---|---|---|---|
| | | | | | |
| | ▓ | | ▓ | | |
| | | | U | | |
| | ▓ | | ▓ | | |
| | ▓ | | ▓ | | |
| | | | | | |

CLAIMS  STRONG  ARMOUR

ENDING  ALMOND  CRADLE

**10–12**

| | | | | | |
|---|---|---|---|---|---|
| | | | | | |
| | ▓ | | ▓ | | ▓ |
| | ▓ | | | | |
| | | | P | | |
| | ▓ | | | | ▓ |

DEEPER  LARGER  BOUNDS

SUDDEN  UDDERS  BUSTLE

Write the four-letter word hidden at the end of one word and the beginning of the next word. The order of the letters may not be changed.

**Example** We had bat<u>s and</u> balls. ___*sand*___

**13** Dad asked me if I knew why our radio was broken. _____

**14** My aunt took her children to the theme park. _____

**15** Deborah's temper got the better of her in class. _____

**16** The police raided one address in Birmingham. _____

From the following information, answer the questions.

The village of Ashley is due north of Calne and due east of the village of Bourne which, in turn, is due north of Dalton. The four villages make the corners of a square.

**17** Which village is west of Ashley? _____

**18** Which village is south of Bourne? _____

**19** Which direction is Calne from Ashley? _____

**20** Which direction is Calne from Bourne? _____

Total [ ]

Test time: 0 ............ 5 ............ 10 minutes

Change the first word into the last word by changing one letter at a time, and making two new, different words in the middle.

**Example** CASE ___CASH___ ___WASH___ WISH

| | | | | |
|---|---|---|---|---|
| **1** | PLAN | _____ | _____ | STAY |
| **2** | TYPE | _____ | _____ | SORE |
| **3** | CLIP | _____ | _____ | CROW |
| **4** | SOUL | _____ | _____ | FOOT |

Which one letter can be added to the front of all of these words to make new words?

**Example** _C_are   _C_at   _C_rate   _C_all   _C_lip

| | | | | | |
|---|---|---|---|---|---|
| **5** | __rain | __lend | __rake | __east | __and |
| **6** | __end | __out | __ever | __earn | __awful |
| **7** | __scent | __maze | __wake | __shore | __jar |
| **8** | __lad | __orge | __amble | __listen | __range |

A B C D E F G H I J K L M N O P Q R S T U V W X Y Z

Fill in the missing symbols, letters or numbers, or underline the words.

**Example** AB is to CD as PQ is to __RS__ .

**9** AZ is to FU as HS is to _____.

**10** ZBE is to GIL as NPS is to _____.

**11** Butterfly is to nectar as (pillowcase, caterpillar, lion) is to (bed, leaf, pillow).

**12** Slow is to tortoise as (flat, brush, fast) is to (hedgehog, pancake, hare).

**13** T17 is to Q20 as L25 is to _____.

**14** ?!£% is to %£!? as @$/; is to _____.

**15** Bow is to arrow as (dart, gun, target) is to (bullet, gun, target).

**16** Speed is to speedometer as (time, race, supersonic) is to (clock, car, jet).

Find and underline the two words that need to change places for each sentence to make sense.

**Example** She went to <u>letter</u> the <u>write</u>.

**17** Guinea-pigs feeds her Sally every day before breakfast.

**18** For lunch today we had roast salad followed by fruit chicken.

**19** I am maths my finding homework hard.

**20** My favourite starts programme television at 8.00pm.

Total

Change the first word of the third pair in the same way as the other pairs to give a new word.

**Example**  bind, hind    bare, hare        but, _hut_

**1**    quiz, quite      flux, flute        plan, _____

**2**    practice, price   stopping, sting   pleasant, _____

**3**    pat, pout       flat, flout        rat, _____

**4**    sludge, slug     fudge, fug        budge, _____

**5**    frame, blame     fright, blight     frown, _____

Look at the pair of words on the left. Underline the one word in the brackets that goes with the word outside the brackets in the same way as the first two words go together.

**Example**  good, better    bad, (naughty, worst, <u>worse</u>, nasty)

**6**    short, tall      wide, (empty, fat, broad, narrow)

**7**    through, around   under, (beneath, over, next, by)

**8**    chatter, babble   talk, (quiet, silent, speak, noise)

**9**    delicate, flimsy   light, (illuminate, heavy, darken, substantial)

**10**   laces, tie       button, (chocolate, fasten, trousers, nose)

A  B  C  D  E  F  G  H  I  J  K  L  M  N  O  P  Q  R  S  T  U  V  W  X  Y  Z

Give the two missing groups of letters and numbers in the following sequences. The alphabet has been written out to help you.

**11**   45      16      ____    20      35      ____    30      28

**12**   4       8       7       ____    ____    14      13      17

**13**   p4      q6      r9      s13     ____    u24     ____    w39

**14**   ACZ     BDY     CEX     DFW     EGV     FHU     ____    ____

**15**   ADb     ____    ILj     MPn     QTr     UXv     YBz     ____    GJh

Look at the first group of three words. The word in the middle has been made from the two other words. Complete the second group of three words in the same way, making a new word in the middle of the group.

**Example**  PAIN    INTO    TOOK        ALSO    _SOON_    ONLY

**16**   SPOT    TOAD    RAID        BOOM    _____    SALT

**17**   CATS    STAB    BILE        BIRD    _____    PINK

**18**   TRIP    PINT    PANT        FEAR    _____    GRID

**19**   SLOW    WOOL    POSH        SLAT    _____    KILL

**20**   TEAM    MEAT    MILE        LEAF    _____    DICE

Total

## From the information supplied, answer the questions.

Naomi, Fern, Husna and Debra are friends at secondary school.

Fern, Naomi and Husna learn Spanish.    Husna, Fern and Debra study French.
Naomi, Husna and Debra study Art.    Debra, Fern and Naomi do Chemistry.
Husna learns Greek.    Fern and Debra do Geography.
Debra and Naomi do Textiles.    Fern and Husna do Music.

**1**  Who does French but does not do Art?    _____

**2**  Who does Chemistry but not Geography?    _____

**3**  Who does Art and Spanish but not Geography or Textiles? _____

**4**  Who does not study Music, Greek or Spanish?    _____

**5**  Who does the fewest subjects?    _____

A  B  C  D  E  F  G  H  I  J  K  L  M  N  O  P  Q  R  S  T  U  V  W  X  Y  Z
The code for the word CANDLE is ECPFNG. Using the same code:

encode these words.

**6**  LIGHT    _____    **7**  DARKNESS    _____

decode these words.

**8**  NWEMA    _____    **9**  ETCBA    _____

Complete the following sentences in the best way by choosing one word from each set of brackets.

**Example**  Tall is to (tree, <u>short</u>, colour) as narrow is to (thin, white, <u>wide</u>).

**10**  Solid is to (jelly, fluid, rigid) as strong is to (liquid, weak, sturdy).

**11**  Thrash is to (scold, burn, defeat) as crush is to (conquer, draw, defy).

**12**  Accurate is to (inaccurate, straight, clever) as true is to (real, genuine, false).

**13**  Hard is to (possible, firm, slim) as coarse is to (dinner, harsh, smooth).

**14**  Modest is to (fashionable, proud, shut) as humble is to (meek, arrogant, lowly).

Write the following letters or words in alphabetical order.

**15**  DRAUGHT _____    **16**  COMPUTER _____

**17**  DREAM    DRAWN    DRAWL    _____

**18**  HEARTH    HEATER    HEARTY    _____

**19**  In alphabetical order, which day of the week comes after Monday? _____

From the information supplied, answer the question.

I appear twice in INCORRUPTIBLE, once in RIDDLE and not at all in PENCIL.

**20**  Which letter is being described? ____

Total

A B C D E F G H I J K L M N O P Q R S T U V W X Y Z

Give the two missing groups of letters and numbers in the following sequences. The alphabet has been written out to help you.

**Example**   CQ    DP    EQ    FP    *GQ*    *HP*

| 1 | 6 | 15 | ___ | ___ | 18 | 9 | 24 | 6 |
|---|---|----|-----|-----|----|----|----|----|
| 2 | ___ | ___ | XCD | WDE | VEF | UFG | TGH | SHI |
| 3 | 60h | 50g | 41f | 33e | 26d | 20c | ___ | ___ |
| 4 | BCa | FGe | JKi | NOm | ___ | VWu | ___ | DEc |

Change the first word into the last word by changing one letter at a time, and making two new, different words in the middle.

**Example**   CASE   *CASH*   *WASH*   WISH

| 5 | WOOD | _____ _____ | WARE | 6 | NOSE | _____ _____ | RICE |
|---|------|---------------|------|---|------|---------------|------|
| 7 | LAZY | _____ _____ | TAME | 8 | MICE | _____ _____ | RISK |
| 9 | PYRE | _____ _____ | SURF | 10 | BEST | _____ _____ | GOAT |
| 11 | PLEA | _____ _____ | FLOW | 12 | COME | _____ _____ | HOST |

Which one letter can be added to the front of all of the words to make new words?

**Example** _Care    _Cat    _Crate    _Call    _Clip

| 13 | __heel | __hat | __all | __hale | __eighty |
|----|--------|-------|-------|--------|----------|
| 14 | __eight | __erring | __eel | __edge | __earth |
| 15 | __otter | __ark | __light | __honey | __rattle |
| 16 | __lope | __at | __bony | __state | __vent |

Eight people went to the theatre. The numbered seats are the ones they have tickets for. Using the information below, work out where each person sat.

Judy sat next to her sister.
Clement sat next to Pravin.
Gretel sat right at the side of the theatre.
Harold sat nearer Kang than anyone else.
Kang sat to the left of Harold.
Sandra sat directly three rows behind Pravin.
Penelope sat diagonally in front of Sandra.

FRONT

STAGE

LEFT    1C 1D    2F 2G    2J    RIGHT

3E

4D 4E

BACK

**17–20**   1C = _____     1D = _____

2F = _____     2G = _____     2J = _____

3E = _____     4D = _____     4E = _____

*Time for a break! Go to Puzzle Page 46* ▶

Total

# Puzzle ①

Take the words and place them in the grid so that each word reads horizontally and vertically.

**Example**

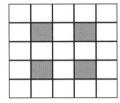

EVERY
BREAD
DOYEN

| B | R | E | A | D |
|---|---|---|---|---|
| R |   | V |   | O |
| E | V | E | R | Y |
| A |   | R |   | E |
| D | O | Y | E | N |

**1**

INLET
PRIZE
ENTER

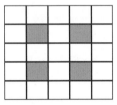

**2**

ENDED
ACRID
AWARE

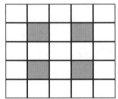

**3**

SALTS
STRAP
LIVER

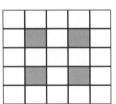

**4**

NEEDS
TAUPE
BATON

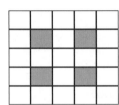

**5**

MEAT    THEN
ACHE    EACH

**6**

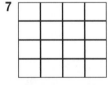

AUNT    DAIS
STOP    INTO

**7**

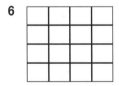

AREA    RARE
PRAY    YEAR

**8**

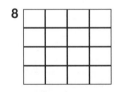

NAME    SIGN
GERM    IDEA

**9**

ALONE
EAGER
GOUDA
ENDED
READS

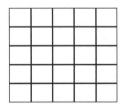

**10**

MEANT
PESTO
THREE
AREAS
STAMP

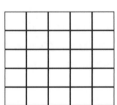

# Puzzle ❷

Help Freddy to jump from one lily-pad to the next by changing one letter at a time.
Watch out! The clues have been mixed up!

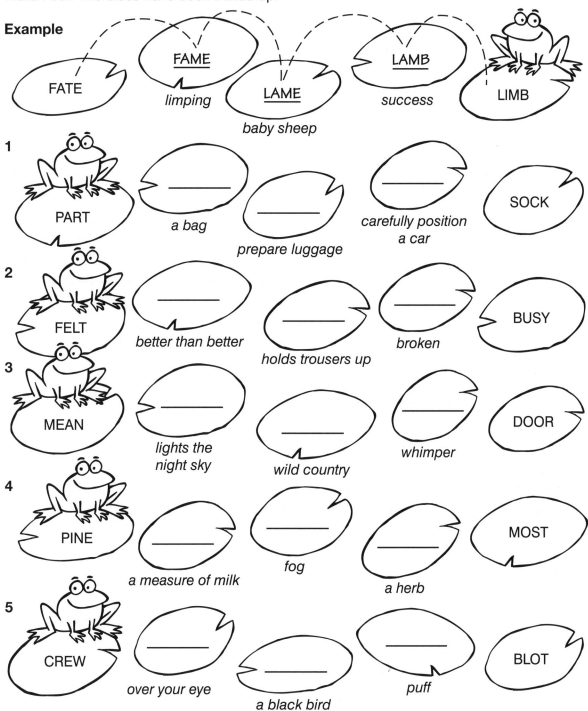

**Example**

FATE → FAME → LAME → LAMB → LIMB

*limping*

*baby sheep*

*success*

**1** PART → ___ → ___ → ___ → SOCK

*a bag*

*prepare luggage*

*carefully position a car*

**2** FELT → ___ → ___ → ___ → BUSY

*better than better*

*holds trousers up*

*broken*

**3** MEAN → ___ → ___ → ___ → DOOR

*lights the night sky*

*wild country*

*whimper*

**4** PINE → ___ → ___ → ___ → MOST

*a measure of milk*

*fog*

*a herb*

**5** CREW → ___ → ___ → ___ → BLOT

*over your eye*

*a black bird*

*puff*

# Puzzle ③

Lucy, Clare, James and Jamila were all taken to Blackpool for a day trip over the summer holidays. Each of them was taken by an older relative. In the afternoon, before they went home, they were allowed one last treat.

From the information below, and using the grid to help you, work out which relative was with each child and what treat each of them chose. Fill in the table at the bottom of the page when you have worked it all out.

|  | mum | grandpa | aunt | sister | funfair | donkey ride | ice cream | beach games |
|---|---|---|---|---|---|---|---|---|
| Lucy |  |  |  |  |  |  |  |  |
| Clare |  |  |  |  |  |  |  |  |
| James |  | ✗ |  |  |  |  |  |  |
| Jamila |  |  |  |  |  |  |  |  |
| funfair |  |  |  |  |
| donkey ride |  |  |  |  |
| ice cream |  |  |  |  |
| beach games |  |  |  |  |

Grandpa sat in a deck-chair while his granddaughter had a donkey ride.

Jamila was frightened of donkeys and did not want to go near them.

Clare was hungry and bought an ice cream with a female relative.

James and his big sister decided not to play beach games.

Mum had great fun playing beach games with her child.

|  | RELATIVE | TREAT |
|---|---|---|
| Lucy |  |  |
| Clare |  |  |
| James |  |  |
| Jamila |  |  |

# Puzzle ④

In the sets of words below, there is a word that links all the other words together.
This word reads vertically down the lightly shaded column of each grid.
The first one has been started for you. Place all the words into each grid
and then read down the lightly shaded column to find your linking word.

| | S | N | O | W | F | L | A | K | E |
|---|---|---|---|---|---|---|---|---|---|

FLOWER   BATHROOM   BARGE   SEASIDE   SNOWFLAKE

**1** The linking word is: _____

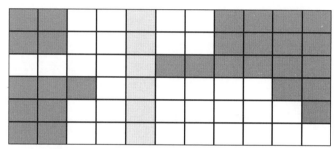

TEETH   DINNER   MUNCHING   ROAST   GRAVY   VEGETABLE

**2** The linking word is: _____

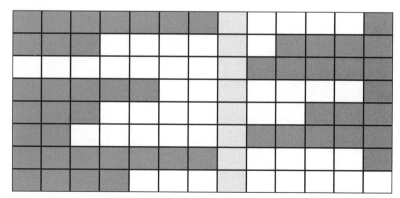

PRISON   COMMA   ARTICLE   ADJECTIVE   STORY
QUESTION   SUBJECT   LETTER

**3** The linking word is: _____

45

# Puzzle ⑤

Using the letters in the star, make as many words as you can. You must use the central letter every time and each letter only once. No two-letter words, initials or proper nouns are allowed. Good luck!

**Example**

| | | | |
|---|---|---|---|
| priest | strip | ripe | sir |
| sprite | | tire | rip |
| | | rest | |

For a good score aim to get: 2 x 6-letter words
8 x 5-letter words
8 x 4-letter words at least!

6-letter words

_____
_____
_____
_____
_____

5-letter words

_____   _____
_____   _____
_____   _____
_____   _____
_____   _____
_____

4-letter words

_____   _____
_____   _____
_____   _____
_____   _____
_____   _____

3-letter words

_____   _____   _____
_____   _____   _____
_____   _____   _____
_____   _____   _____
_____   _____   _____

# Progress Grid

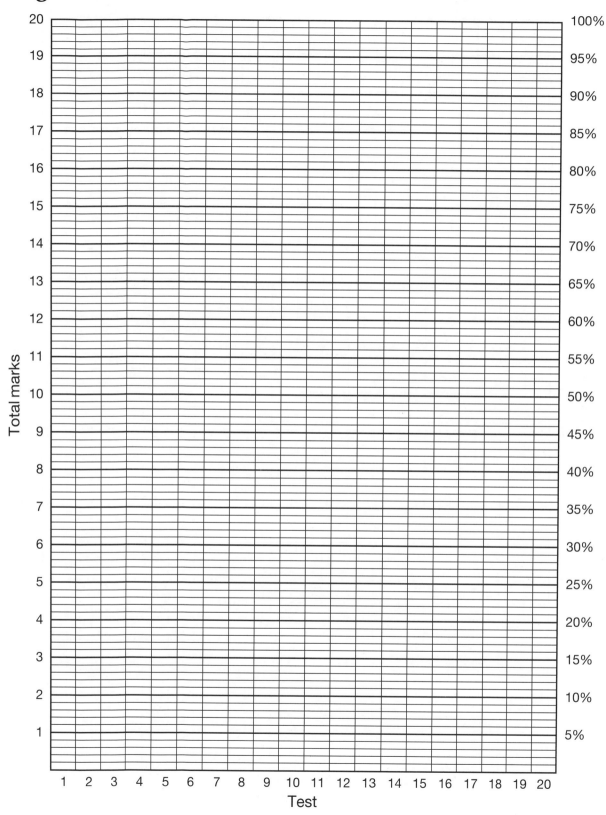

# Progress Grid

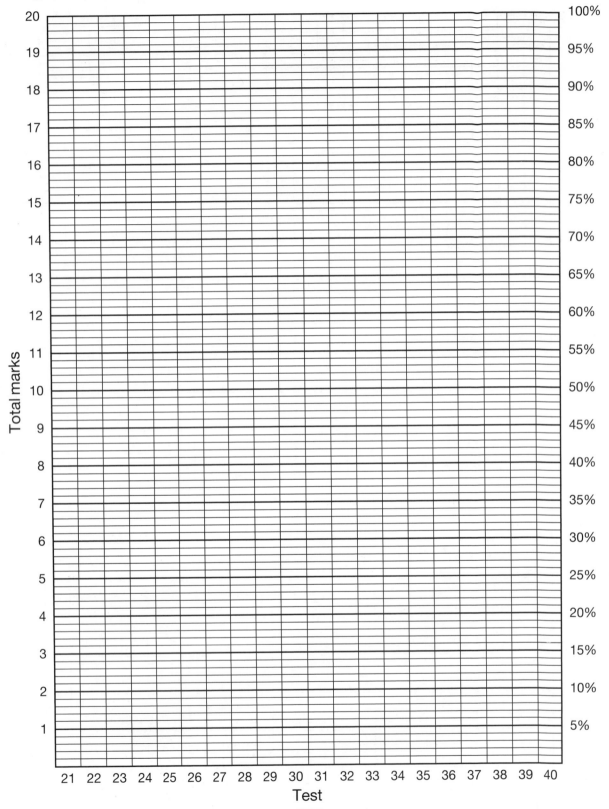